Beginnings

Spiritual Formation For Leaders

Beginnings

Spiritual Formation for Leaders

Dwight L. Grubbs

BEGINNINGS: SPIRITUAL FORMATION FOR LEADERS

FIRST EDITION
Copyright © 1994 by
Dwight L. Grubbs

Scripture quotations are from the *Revised Standard Version of the Bible*, copyrighted 1946, 1952, (c), 1971, 1973, by the Division of Christian Education of the National Council of the Churches of Christ in the USA. Used by permission.

Library of Congress Catalog Card Number: 93-73485

7985 / ISBN 1-55673-586-3   PRINTED IN U.S.A.

Dedication

This is a book for "beginners." It is dedicated to ministers just starting out, to those beginning a new phase of ministry, and to those answering the call to lay ministry.

To answer a call is an awesome decision. Leadership is demanding. Deep commitment is needed in order to meet the nearly impossible expectations. As you read, remember that I will be praying for you. You have my respect and appreciation for your decision. Our great Shepherd will help you become the person you yearn to be.

If you're entering into ministry as a vocation, I feel a strong kinship with you. Professional training — liberal arts college, Bible college, or Seminary — demands special discipline. Keep at it. For those launching a ministry without formal preparation, my hope is that this book will contribute to your continuing education.

To you, my brothers and sisters in ministry, clergy and lay, this book is lovingly dedicated.

Dwight L. Grubbs
Anderson, Indiana

Artist, Sylvia Grubbs

Table Of Contents

Acknowledgements

To write a book is to share one's life. This book is part of my spiritual pilgrimage. I have been extremely aware of a "great cloud of witnesses" who have been my companions along the way. I would like to give special thanks to a few of them.

To my parents, Rev. and Mrs. J. C. Grubbs who in 54 years of pastoral ministry, provided for me a model of faithfulness.

To Sylvia, my wife of 34 years, who has brought a joy to my life, and a depth to our shared spiritual pilgrimage, for which I am eternally grateful.

To my wife's parents, Rev. M. W. and Rev. Lolita Kennedy whose lives and ministries have inspired me, and who provided a comfortable place with a spectacular view of the mountains in Chromo, Colorado, in order to reflect and write.

To my faith community, the Church of God (Anderson, Indiana) which nurtured me, provided opportunities for leadership, ordained me, and forgives my foibles; and to the congregations that loved me and called me "pastor."

To the Administration of the School of Theology, Anderson University (Anderson, Indiana) for the sabbatical leave which afforded the time for most of the research and writing that went into this book; and to Joyce Krepshaw for typing the manuscript.

To the educational institutions that guided my quest for knowledge (Quachita High School, Northeast Louisiana University, both in Monroe, Louisiana; Anderson School of Theology, Asbury Theological Seminary, and Texas Christian University); and to Mid-America Bible College (formerly Gulf-Coast Bible College), where I was first called "professor."

To Dr. Boyce Blackwelder, Dr. Irene Caldwell, Dr. Donald Johnson, Dr. Robert E. Coleman, Dr. William R. Hammond, and Miss Sallie L. Humble, who are but representative of the many teachers who prodded me toward excellence, invited my questions, and nudged me to develop my faith.

Introduction

Before you go farther in this book, let me say a few things that I hope will help you make the best use of it. I think it might be useful for you to know something of my perspectives, and my hopes for you as you read.

First, understand that this will be a rather personal book. I invite you to **experience** it with me. You have probably noticed that I am using personal pronouns. I will try to write as though I am talking directly to you. And, periodically, I will invite your response.

Second, let me suggest that you **not** try to read the book straight through quickly, but that you approach it more deliberately. It might help if you keep a notebook or journal handy. Record insights, concerns for reflection and prayer, and questions for research. Now and then, I'll suggest exercises, questions, Scriptures, or ideas for additional reflection and writing. I will invite you to evaluate your spiritual life, learn some new approaches to growth and ministry, and generally explore your life ''in Christ.''

Third, it might help for me to define what I mean when I mention ''ministry,'' ''pastor,'' ''minister,'' or ''pastoral ministry.'' I likely will use the terms somewhat interchangeably, rather than precisely. ''Ministry'' is that servanthood to which all believers have been summoned. It is done by the laity as well as by the ordained.

I understand "pastor" to be the professional designation for persons who enter ministry as a vocation, or profession, or calling. Thus, a pastor is, generally, an ordained person who functions as pastor in a local congregation. (Also, pastors have been known to become chaplains, associates in a congregation, administrators, teachers, counselors, and the list could go on). Thus, ministry is what clergy persons and lay persons **do**.

So, generally, when I refer to ministers and ministry, I'm thinking of Christian leaders both pastors and the laity. This book is designed to assist persons to anticipate, examine, prepare for, continue in, or, perhaps, make major changes in ministry. In short, this book is for leaders who are seeking after God in order to find guidance, hope and assurance.

I deeply appreciate God's called ministers. They are the heart of the church. So, whether you are lay or ordained, I trust that you will profit from your interaction with this book. Especially, if you're a "beginner"! I hope that you'll find some bread for your journey into Christ and into ministry.

The motivation for writing this book is my concern, that, many evangelical protestant pastors are quite well prepared in terms of **knowing** (history, theology, Bible) and **doing** (homiletics, counseling, administration) but are sometimes lacking in terms of **being** (self-awareness, personal integrity, spirituality). There has been a neglect of the inner life, in my observation, among protestant ministerial educational institutions and judicatories, as well as among the individual ministers. Leaders are often more motivated to action than to prayer.

My experience as a seminarian, and as a seminary professor since 1978, is that we'd rather **do** most anything than to pray and listen to God. I hope that statement is not too harsh nor inaccurate. I have observed that college students, seminarians, and ministers often enjoy engaging in scholarly discussions, exegesis, research and the like. But to spend significant amounts of time in prayer and the devotional study of the Bible, appear too passive. We prefer to be active in the work of God.

And now the thesis of the book: Effective ministry requires the establishment of a vital spiritual center.

In 1973, when I began teaching applied theology courses at Gulf-Coast Bible College, I drew a triangle on the board one day to depict what I consider to be the basics of effective ministry.

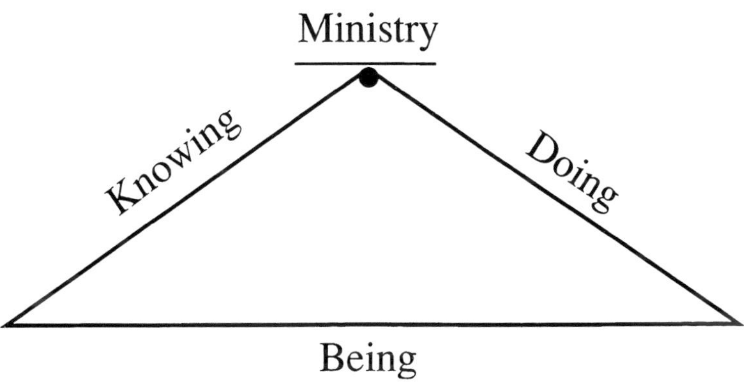

My statement to the class went something like this: In order to be effective as a minister, you need to **know** some things, be able to **do** some things, but most important of all, you need to **be** a certain kind of person. Since then, I've drawn a lot of triangles, and tried to convey the same basic message.

What I have been trying to say is that quality of one's life "in Christ" (being) is the foundation upon which knowledge and skills can be added in order to support an effective ministry. I believe that **being** is the source which sustains that ministry.

What do you think? Do you agree that our spirituality is as essential as our knowledge and skills? How important is being — or becoming — to you, as you begin ministry?

To be concerned about becoming is to be grappling with such questions as these:

What kind of person am I?
What kind of person do I want to become?
What do I want to do with my life?
To whom and to what will I pledge my loyalty?
What do I believe about God?
What is my relationship with God?
How do I propose to serve my community and my world?

It should be obvious that true spirituality is a blend of interior and exterior concerns. The challenge that always faces us is that of harmonizing the two concerns. The church has tended to err by moving toward one extreme or the other. An enduring and satisfying spirituality demands that we discover that delicate balance, live whole (holy) lives, even as we seek to help others grow.

A spirituality for ministry is infinitely more than being subjectively preoccupied with one's inner processes. On the other hand, ministry is more than knowing and doing. To be busy and informed is admirable. But to allow the "busyness" of life to hinder spiritual development is tragic. A spirituality for the long haul requires looking both inwardly and outwardly.

Let me now indicate some of the perspectives that I hold, which have influenced what I have written. I'm sure there are other biases, some of which I'm scarcely aware, but these are noted in order to help you know some of my viewpoints.

First, I write with the perspective that effective ministry requires a life-changing encounter with Jesus Christ, which is salvation by faith through grace, and includes a deep commitment to a Christian lifestyle, obedience to the Word of God, and loyalty to the church.

Second, I write with the perspective that ministry is a calling. For me, the call is an experience — personal, impelling, and transforming. In this charismatic experience, one senses a divine summons to ministry, and with that sense, there is an awareness of authority, gifting, guidance, and community. Included is the call to preparation.

Third, I write with the perspective that when presenting ourselves for ordination, the most important vow we could take would be the commitment to inner transformation. It would be a vow that consecrates the ego, and affirms dependence upon God — "not I, but Christ who lives in me" (Galatians 2:20).

Thus, ordination means first of all the entering into a relationship with the Spirit, for the growth and development of the pastor's soul. Only secondarily is it a partnership for the advancement of the Kingdom. This is not to say that spiritual formation is a process of self-absorption. It **is** to say, however, that one cannot give what one does not have.

Fourth, I write with the perspective that Christian leaders tend to err on the side of works righteousness. A high-energy, success-oriented, program-centered ministry often seems to be the ideal. The typical pastor frequently doesn't have the time nor the inclination to retreat, relax, and pray. We are tough on ourselves and often fail to claim God's grace for our humanness. I can remember about 30 years ago at a clergy conference, hearing that "the successful pastor finds ways to keep the lights on at the church building every night of the week." Am I the only one who ever heard that advice?

Fifth, I write with the perspective that spirituality is more struggle than it is celebration. There is great joy and fulfillment while on the pilgrimage. But one never reaches a state of accomplishment, when it is time to hold a final victory celebration. And while we struggle, we are keenly conscious that long ago God chose us. Long before we knew anything about struggle or celebration, grace was available. And it still is! So we never count ourselves as having apprehended, but we press on, realizing that the journey is our home.

Sixth, I write with the perspective that there are tremendous possibilities of joy, strength, peace, and love, awaiting the minister who intentionally enters the deeper life quest. I am not talking about pious, affected, sentimental posturing. True spirituality doesn't result in a sort of saccharin religious demeanor that we put on, so that others can spot us as ministers from a mile off. But, internally, the qualities of the Christ-like life are there, embryonic perhaps, but becoming.

Seventh, I write with the perspective that the goal of the spiritual journey is not necessarily religious satisfaction, nor personal fulfillment, nor some kind of individual experiential ecstasy. Though it may result in any or all of these, the ultimate objective is that we contribute vigor and hope and service to the Body of Christ, the church, which then makes this new life available to the whole world. God's best love letter to the world is a church composed of spiritual people. Our calling is to become just one letter of the alphabet in that divine message, or perhaps, by His grace, one word fitly placed and full of meaning for some needy soul.

To conclude this Introduction, let me make four suggestions for the reading of this book.

1. Try to set aside a half hour or so at a time for uninterrupted, unhurried reading, reflecting, and writing. Approach your reading in a relaxed, contemplative mood, preferably only a few pages at a time.

2. Secure a notebook that will become something of a journal for you. In it, record responses to the book, as well as other thoughts, feelings, ideas, or information that relate to your experiences with the book.

3. If possible, work through the book with your spiritual friend, or a small sharing group. Ministerial self-assessment, growth-planning, and prayer are best undertaken in community.

4. Keep in mind that we're all "beginners." That's what grace is all about! Ministry is full of beginnings. And starting over leads to new accomplishments, renewal, and life.

May your labor with this book bring significant rewards!

17

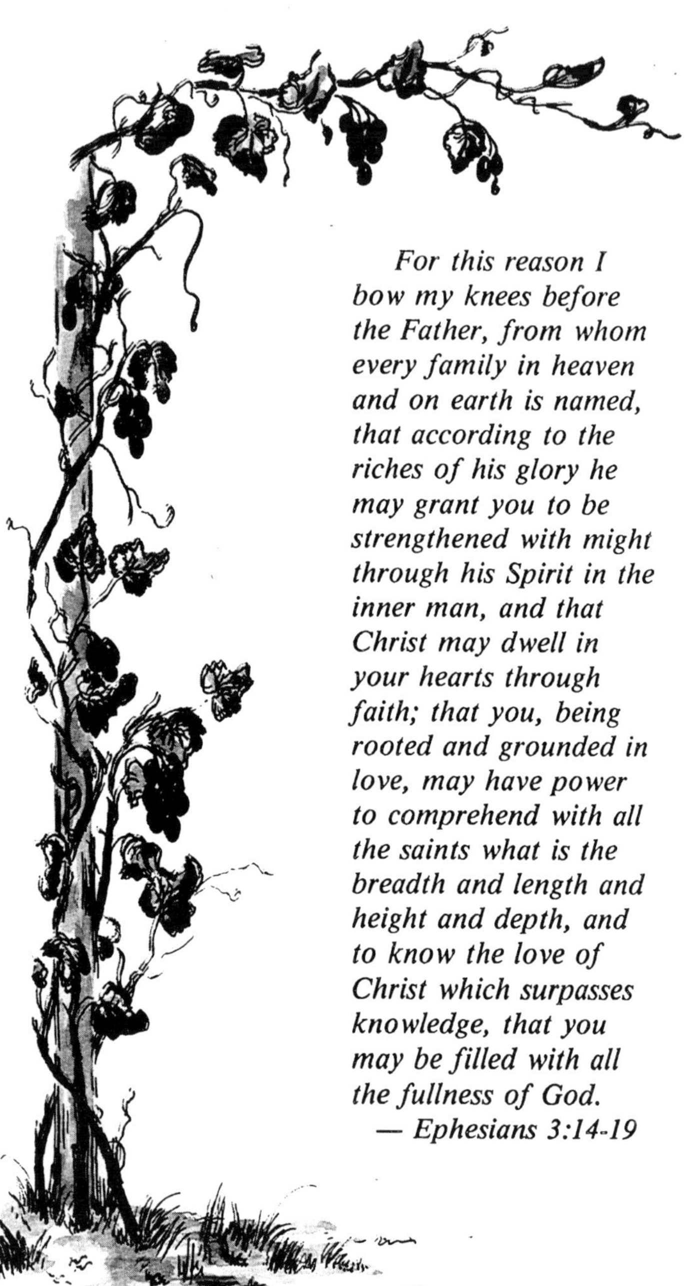

For this reason I
bow my knees before
the Father, from whom
every family in heaven
and on earth is named,
that according to the
riches of his glory he
may grant you to be
strengthened with might
through his Spirit in the
inner man, and that
Christ may dwell in
your hearts through
faith; that you, being
rooted and grounded in
love, may have power
to comprehend with all
the saints what is the
breadth and length and
height and depth, and
to know the love of
Christ which surpasses
knowledge, that you
may be filled with all
the fullness of God.
— Ephesians 3:14-19

*I am the true vine,
and my Father is the
vinedresser. Abide in
me, and I in you. As
the branch cannot bear
fruit by itself, unless it
abides in the vine,
neither can you, unless
you abide in me. I am
the vine, you are the
branches. He who
abides in me, and I in
him, he it is that bears
much fruit, for apart
from me you can do
nothing.*
— John 15:1, 4-5

I

Foundations

For no other foundation can anyone lay than that
which is laid, which is Jesus Christ (1 Corinthians 3:11).

Frank W. Gunsaulus, pastor of Central Church in Chicago, delivered the Lyman Beecher Lectures at Yale Divinity School in the spring of 1911. His subject was the minister and the spiritual life. The following brief excerpt illustrates the basic theme of his lectures, and speaks powerfully to our own day:

> *I shall not recommend spirituality, but I will begin with the understanding between us that, without it, the breath of life is not in the nostrils of the minister of Christ ... The spiritual life alone has in it the hope and process of man's becoming and being. It is, therefore, the experience of God likeness. As being is deeper than doing, it is to the perennial Fountain of all worthy doing that I come at once (Gunsaulus, 1911, p. 14).*

As stated in the Introduction, the primary purpose of this book is to provide some guidance and encouragement for persons who are seeking to build a spirituality for effective ministry. Let's begin with foundations. We will consider three basic questions: Why spiritual formation? What is spiritual formation? How may we begin to understand spiritual formation?

I. Why Spiritual Formation?

I will not attempt an elaborate rationale for spiritual formation. However, the serious student will find abundant material on the subject elsewhere. In the Bible, especially from the life of Jesus, from church history, and from biographies, one may find teachings and models of spiritual growth. Nevertheless, let me give several reasons for entering into intentional spiritual formation in a disciplined manner. ("Discipline" will be discussed more fully in Chapter 2.) For the believer on pilgrimage, spiritual formation will significantly assist persons in:

1. The disciplined worship of God. Worship should not be arbitrary nor casual, but should represent our best, most focused efforts in praise, prayer and worship.

2. The disciplined development of character and lifestyle. This might be called our "commitment to holiness" (Jones, 1985).

3. The disciplined discernment of vocation. A call to ministry, like salvation, is dynamic. Thus, a vocation is always subject to review and revision.

4. The disciplined discovery, understanding, and use of spiritual gifts. An honest appraisal of the gifts with which the Holy Spirit has equipped us will add to our self-understanding, self-confidence, and effectiveness in ministry.

5. The disciplined discharge of duties in ministry. It behooves us to know what our duties are, and to avoid the tendency of attempting to meet the often unrealistic expectations of others, or ourselves.

6. The disciplined establishment and nurturance of loving relationships with family, friends, and acquaintances.

7. The disciplined expression of prophetic ministries to the larger world, in support of human services, peace, justice, and renewal.

From this list, it should be obvious that spiritual formation has to do with all of life. Spirituality must never be isolated in an obscure corner of our lives. Rather, it is foundational and inclusive. Spiritual formation, then, is not only an academic subject to be discussed objectively. It is a process to be understood, entered into and nurtured. My task in writing is to describe the process and to offer encouragement.

II. What Is Spiritual Formation?

What do we mean by the term spiritual formation? We might say that Christian spiritual formation is an intentional, continuous movement toward a whole life in Christ, coupled with a conscious receptivity to the work of the Spirit in us.

Spiritual formation is not so much something done to persons, nor even something done by persons. Rather, it is something voluntarily entered into, in partnership with God, to the end that one is shaped, equipped, inspired, for life and ministry, and God becomes more present to the individual. While the process seems to work best when one volunteers for it, there are some occasions when, for example, clergy candidates are required to enter a formation program as part of an educational or ordination track.

John Wesley suggested that spiritual formation is not seeking new ways to discover God, nor working harder to make God real to us. Rather, it is living in such a way as not to resist God's gracious initiatives. Put very simply, it is paying loving attention to all of God that we know, with all of our selves that we can, using all the resources that we can gather.

The story of spiritual formation is the story of humankind's quest to know God and to be known by God. It began with the creation, when the Creator put that God-shaped vacuum within each of us, and we were destined to be restless, until we find our rest in God.

Spiritual formation, then, is a rather general term used to describe the process of becoming, growing, maturing, or developing in Godliness. It has sociological, psychological, theological, emotional, physical, missional, relational, cognitive, and intuitive implications. Did I leave anything out? In short, spiritual formation has to do with the development of the whole person.

Each of us is created unique, called to transforming union in relationship with God. According to Nemeck and Coombs, "We are to return to the Father, with His Son, in the Holy Spirit" (Nemeck and Coombs, 1985, p. 15). The process of this return journey may be called spiritual formation. Let me say again:

The thesis of this book is that effective ministry requires the establishment of a vital spiritual center. Another way of saying this is: The only valid integrating center for ministry is the minister's life in Christ.

The intentional building of that center, may be called spiritual formation. To make the concept very practical, let me offer a list of what I believe one must bring to spiritual formation (what one must *intend to do*), meanwhile, trusting the Holy Spirit to do the deeper work of transformation:

1. An inner hunger to know and to be known by God (the Pilgrim's motivation).

2. A vital association with a worshipping community of believers (the Pilgrim's connection with the Body of Christ).

3. A program of devotional disciplines (the Pilgrim's source of heart-nourishment).

4. A commitment to scholarly study and reflection (the Pilgrim's source of mind-nourishment).

5. An intentional relationship with a spiritual friend (the Pilgrim's accountability).

6. An involvement in service and social ministries (the Pilgrim's mission).

7. An attitude of humility (the Pilgrim's posture and practice).

Balance is essential. To omit any one would be injurious to spiritual health. To become obsessed with any one might result in a sort of spiritual fanaticism.

Morton Kelsey suggests that a growing Christian experience is the goal of spiritual formation. He provides a list of five requirements (with credit to Friedrich von Huegel for part of the list) that need to be met, in order to be moving toward the goal of maturity:

1. It is necessary to have a religious tradition that has been revealed in history and refined through institutional practice.

2. It requires openness to and cultivation of direct experience of God.

3. It requires the development of our rational faculties, our capacity for critical, analytical thought.

4. We need knowledge of the nature of the human psyche and how it operates internally, and in interaction with the world and other human beings.

5. We need to learn how to care for each other, how to love (Kelsey, 1983, p. 32).

Lest there be any confusion, let me say very clearly that spiritual formation and spiritual direction are not the same. Formation is the larger process; direction helps to facilitate that process. Formation is a process-goal, while direction is a means to that goal. Chapter 3 will describe the practice of spiritual direction, and perhaps, add clarity.

III. How may we begin to understand spiritual formation?

There are two aspects of the subject that we need to examine. Our approach will be to consider first the theological and historical development of Christian spirituality. This should help us to see that we are dealing with a concern that has deep roots in the beliefs and traditions of the church.

Secondly, we will consider the practice of spiritual formation. Ideas and suggestions will be provided to encourage persons in their quest to know God and to be known by Him. Suggestions for additional reading may be found in the bibliography.

A. *Theological and Historical Foundations*

Thomas Oden, in writing about the necessity of a theology for ministry, says,

> *It is dangerous to the health of the church for ministry to be practiced without good foundation in Scripture and tradition, reason and experience (Oden, 1983, p. xii).*

I agree with Oden, and suggest that the same statement needs to be made in reference to spiritual formation. Without adequate biblical, theological, historical, and experiential foundations, we easily fall prey to tangents or, perhaps, heresies. To help prevent spiritual formation from becoming another religious fad, let us examine some foundations.

Salvation

The most fundamentally persistent questions of the human heart have to do with God: Who is God? How is it with God and me? Am I at peace in God's world? What about the hereafter?

Of course those questions are framed in many different ways, depending on theological perspective and cultural setting. Religious satisfaction (for the Christian) is generally defined in terms of some sort of experiential relationship with God. From the beginning of the Christian era, persons have sought a satisfying relationship with God.

Though experiential salvation is more than feelings (after all, there are historical facts, revelation, doctrine, and reason involved here), it is also more than intellectual assent.

The history of Christian salvation may be superficially and briefly described in this manner: From Jesus' time to the Middle Ages, there was a delicate balance between experiential and rational Christianity. Under the influence of Aquinas, the Renaissance, and the scientific movement, there was a trend toward rationalism (an intellectual faith).

Periodically there have been a number of expressions of ''heart-felt religion'' (mysticism and revivalism, as examples) as persons sought for satisfying faith. At the present time, there seems to be a growing interest in the deeper life. This may be in reaction both to fundamentalism (with its emphasis upon doctrinal correctness) and to liberalism (with its emphasis upon good works).

It seems that, in recent years, we more frequently use terms like ''born again,'' or ''saved.'' At least we hear it often on television. I sincerely trust that the frequent use is not an indication of trivialization. The great doctrine of salvation is one of the major tenets of the Christian faith. It is supremely an experience, and it follows that we speak of it in an experiential vocabulary.

Spiritual Theology

Spiritual formation has its primary roots and connections in *spiritual theology*, which is the classical academic discipline to which we turn in order to find the origin, development, and practice of spiritual formation. Spiritual theology is the term generally used to indicate what formerly was called ascetical or mystical theology. Sometimes, the terms spiritual theology and experiential theology are used interchangeably. The term "formation theology" is currently being used, especially by Adrian van Kaam and Susan Muto, to refer to intentional spiritual development.

Spiritual theology has to do with Christ's redemptive work in the individual soul. It is concerned with what constitutes the spiritual life, and how one can advance in the pursuit of it. Spiritual theology seeks to make known the ways that persons can participate in the mysteries of God, and, thus, become in union with God. It has for its end to teach persons how, and to guide persons in, the process of becoming holy. Thus, it is a functional science, and, in a sense, fits more naturally into an alliance with practical or applied theology, than with systematic theology or Christian doctrine.

Perhaps an aside is in order here, to set "spiritual theology" in the broader context of Christian belief. We have traditionally defined theology as having three strands. (1) Systematic or dogmatic theology focuses on theology as sure knowledge, and seeks to understand, explain, and teach the mysteries of God, and lead persons to a (mainly) cognitive acceptance of ideas or beliefs. As the science of the study of God, it has been called the "queen of sciences." (2) Moral theology focuses on what needs to be done, or not done, in order to avoid sin, and live a life pleasing to God. Charges of "legalism" or "behavior modification'' are sometimes directed at the conclusions of moral theologians. (3) Spiritual theology (see definition on previous page or further discussions later).

This all too-brief characterization of three "types" of theology is not intended to emphasize the differences, but to call for understanding and balance. *A healthy theology upon which one may build a rationale for spiritual formation, needs to have balanced proportions of doctrinal, moral, and experiential components.* Indeed, one might suspect that a theology is inadequate which does not contain appropriate elements of each of the three types of theology.

On this issue of our dangerous tendency to dichotomize spirituality, Thomas Merton said,

> *Dogmatic and mystical theology, or theology and spirituality, are not to be set apart in mutually exclusive categories, as if mysticism were for saintly women and theological study were for practical, but alas, unsaintly men. This fallacious division perhaps explains much that is actually lacking both in theology and spirituality. But the two belong together. Unless they are united there is no fervor, no life and no spiritual value in theology, no substance, no meaning and no sure orientation in contemplative life (Merton, 1972, pp. 197-198).*

So, when I speak of rooting spiritual formation in the soil of spiritual theology, I am speaking of a theology that has a good balance of biblical understanding, an awareness of church history and historical theology, a grasp of the psycho-social insights from the behavioral sciences, plus an openness to religious experience, and a sensitivity to our mandate to evangelize and to work for social justice. To be involved in the "outer world" of work and ministry, without proper attention to the "inner world" of devotion and personal growth, is to risk vocational disaster. My fear is that we deepen the split between the two "worlds." My hope is that we keep the two in dynamic tension, but intimate inter-relatedness.

Mysticism and Asceticism

Historically, the two main streams that converged into Christian spiritual theology are mysticism and asceticism. In a few words, mysticism may be defined as the belief that one comes to know God by putting oneself before God in open receptivity to what God would do in the soul. An experience of union with God is the objective, and it is achieved largely by quietly waiting.

Asceticism may be defined as the belief that one comes to know God by working at it, by practicing the disciplines of self-denial and separation. An experience of union with God is the objective, and it is achieved largely by human effort.

Both styles of spirituality gained early popularity and widespread practice in the church, especially in the monastic movement. Most historians think that mysticism and asceticism emerged in the church primarily as reactions *against* evil, and as efforts *toward* holiness. During the first four or five centuries of the Christian era, an extremely pagan world, the influx into the church of large numbers of unregenerate followers, and the institutionalizing of the church, caused many persons to react against established religion in particular, and society in general. As a result, many sincere believers fled to the deserts and some formed monasteries, hoping to avoid sin and religious corruption. Others made similar flights, but their pilgrimage was more in quest of interior holiness, peace, and creativity. And, of course, some had both concerns as objectives.

In this brief overview, I have in mind several hundred years of church history, development, and change, so it is necessary to speak in general terms. But from the beginning of Christianity (New Testament times) to the present, an identifiable movement (usually called mysticism, pietism, or evangelicalism) has kept alive the notion that a personal, experiential relationship with Jesus Christ is normative for the believer.

In order to make mysticism and asceticism a little more contemporary, one might say that a *modern* mystic is a believer. Such a person is open to the unexplainable workings of God, and experiences a direct communion with God. A mystic does not need rational proofs in order to maintain faith. A *modern* ascetic is one who denies self in such ways as living simply. Such a person is less success oriented and more service oriented. An ascetic does not need the world's approval in order to maintain faith.

Historical Foundations

From the time of the Desert Fathers (c. 200-500 A.D.) to the present there have been multitudes of persons who believed that humankind has a special kinship with God, and that God can be known, worshipped, obeyed, experienced, and loved. These pioneers in Christian spirituality, from Anthony to E. Stanley Jones, shared their conviction that there could be an immediate and intuitive relationship with God, quite apart from the sacramental and ecclesiastical superintendency of the church, and sometimes even in conflict with the church.

Augustine (354-430), Bernard of Clairvaux (1090-1153), Francis of Assisi (1182-1226), Meister Eckhart (1260-1327), Jan van Ruysbroeck (1293-1381), and Erasmus (1466-1536), were each significantly influential upon Martin Luther (1483-1546), as he developed his views upon spiritual formation. Luther along with these and other leaders sought for reform within the Catholic church, specifically with regard to the experiential (mystical) way to salvation, as different from the sacramental way. But their views contributed more to the Protestant Reformation than to the Roman Reformation, and many of their views on personal salvation have come down to us by way of the movement called pietism.

My purpose here is not to give a detailed treatment of the development of spiritual formation in the church. However, in Chapter III, I will return to a brief history of spiritual direction, on the assumption that many Protestant Christians are not very familiar with this part of our heritage.

Rationalism

It is unfortunate that many of our contemporary protestant educational institutions are strongly influenced by a rationalistic-materialistic world view that provides little place for spiritual reality. This can be traced, according to Morton Kelsey, back to late medieval times when Aristotelian philosophy became dominant. In essence, it held that human beings could have no direct contact with the spiritual world, and that reality is apprehended by the five senses, plus reason, which comes into play when the five senses are inadequate. Aristotle doubted the existence of any reality not discovered by reason and the sensory experience. These beliefs became a part of Catholic and Protestant scholasticism and the enlightenment.

This "scientific spirit" became "truth," and the spiritual world was "illusion." The ideas of scientific rationalism, having received the endorsement of many protestant theologians, including Barth, Bultmann, and Brunner (Kelsey, 1983, pp. 13-14), has been perpetuated by liberalism, modernism, and humanism.

On this issue of the increase within the church of a rationalistic-materialistic world view, along with the decrease of a mystical-experiential theology, Louis Bouyer writes as follows:

> *When mysticism is under discussion, the theologians of these schools (Barth, Bultmann, the neo-Lutherans) — while unable to deny that there have been mystics throughout the whole of Protestantism, and different as their respective positions are — have been completely united in their insistence that where true Protestantism is concerned, mysticism is the most unacceptable reality of all (Bouyer, 1969, p. 57).*

Given that observation by Bouyer, and aware of the "weight" of Barth, Bultmann, Brunner, Nygren, Ebeling, and others, I still insist that mysticism, asceticism, spiritual theology, grace gifts, theocratic leadership, and experiential faith be given their rightful places in the belief system and the practices of the church. What I am praying for is a great surge of emphasis upon spiritual formation that will enable us to move beyond defending doctrinal positions, or debating theological formulations, beyond a mainly intellectual approach to the Christian faith, all the way to that place where persons experience a dynamic, personal relationship with a living God.

When God's called ministers are transformed, energized, and directed by the Holy Spirit, as part of an intentional spiritual formation regimen, then there is hope for the church, the ministers will find fulfillment, and God's will on earth will be accomplished. And in order to encounter the living God in this manner, one needs to be open to the validity of Christian experience, and affirm that the mystical way to God is an acceptable approach to reality.

B. *Foundations for the Practice of Spiritual Formation*

Two concerns need our consideration. Foundational to the practice of spiritual formation, are the issues of relatedness and process.

Relatedness

To become involved in the practice of spiritual formation is to become involved with people. Spiritual formation is primarily a relationship, or more accurately, a combination of relationships. The individualist will run into difficulty at this point. Spiritual "loners" will avoid intimacy, disclosure, and spiritual direction.

My hunch is that some persons enter professional ministry with an innate urge to be leaders — "king of the hill," if you please. This urge is a valid one, and leaders are needed in the church. But this same drive for leadership (authority) also frequently causes persons to have difficulty working with boards or judicatories, or supervisors.

Good leaders often make poor followers! And how can one be "king of the hill" and still answer to a committee, or share honestly with a prayer group, or seek spiritual direction? This whole area of interpersonal relationships and the minister is a delicate and troublesome one, and we cannot deal with it here fully. In passing, however, let it be said that if one is aware of a strong resistance toward the whole idea of close relationships with others, has difficulty working with persons in authority, and fears any experience that approaches self-disclosure, then ministry will likely be difficult. I think such a person should seek personal counseling before continuing in ministry.

Perhaps the major motivation for spiritual formation is the persistent "ideal image," which has been a part of the Christian tradition since apostolic times. This "ideal image" holds that it is possible for the sincere seeker to experience:

1. Union with God (The Vision)
2. Imitation of Christ (The Way)
3. Life in the Spirit (Continuous Grace)

The obvious implication is that the person being spiritually formed can have a dynamic relationship with the three Persons of the Trinity. Also, as part of the "ideal image," there is an "ideal praxis," which insists on a healthy balance between one's experience with God and one's service to God and the whole inhabited earth. Thus, piety and good works are to be held in vigorous tension as one seeks to know, to do, and to be.

In Old Testament times, the concepts of Father-God, Messiah, and the covenant, each in its own way, provided powerful metaphors of the God who longed for vital relationships with people. This relationship with God is illustrated in the life of Abraham, who,

> *obeyed when he was called to go out to a place which he was to receive as an inheritance; and he went out, not knowing where he was to go. By faith he sojourned in the land of promise ... (Hebrews 11:8-9).*

About all Abraham knew was that he had gotten directions from God, he had made a commitment to obey, and that he would not take lightly the covenant he had made with God. So Abraham went into partnership. His life is a story of one man's personal relationship with God. Abraham provides an excellent case study in intentional spiritual formation.

Jesus provided a model in the first program of Christian spiritual formation, when he called some men, "to be with Him" (Mark 3:13-14). He then spent much of his valuable time with them, preparing them for life and for ministry.

Frequently, Jesus went alone to pray (Mark 1:35) and invited His disciples to do likewise (Mark 3:13; 6:32). When Jesus went into the wilderness (His desert experience, one might say), He went because the Spirit led Him there (Matthew 4:1) for a time of preparation.

A careful study of Jesus' wilderness experience will show that it was an intensely dialogical and relational event. However, preachers and theologians frequently insist on extracting doctrines and sermons from the event, without giving due regard to the powerfully personal nature of the story.

Bruce Larson, writing about relational theology, declares that, "the Bible deals primarily with relationships and only indirectly with doctrine." He says that our task as ministers is not to, "make people believe the right things, so much as enabling them to experience a relationship with God and with one another" (Larson, 1971, pp. 16-17). Spiritual formation is a very relational adventure, involving our total selves, God, and significant other persons, at the deepest levels.

The priesthood of believers is a doctrine that needs to be taught and practiced. Unfortunately, many pastors tend to view ministry as something done *to* or done *for* people, when in fact it is best understood as something done *with* them.

We Really Do Need Each Other, is the title of an excellent little book by Reuben Welch. But it is more than the title of a book — it is a statement of philosophy about ministry that, I think, holds a great deal of promise. When we decide that ministry is best done in context — as part of a team, in cooperation with a congregation, as members of the family of God — then we have linked our hearts and hands to each other and to God, so that our ministry can proceed, and our efforts can be effective. We really should not try to go it alone, but together — relationally.

Process

Process suggests that there is a beginning point, that there are goals, and that there are procedures, but that spiritual formation is never really finished. We are becomers, but we never totally become. There is always a need for more growth, insight, cultivation of gifts, development of maturity. In ministry, one is made painfully aware of the fact of process. To become adequate in one area, is to be faced with the challenge of becoming equipped in another. One of the realities of vocation is that one is always "getting ready."

Perhaps this process approach to the Christian life is troublesome for those who view salvation, sanctification, and spirituality (for example) more in terms of doctrine, law, reason, and state of being, than in terms of relationships, experience, and becoming. I am not suggesting that salvation and sanctification are not crisis experiences. I believe that one cannot ooze one's way into the Body of Christ! Nevertheless, after a decision (involving reason and faith) to follow Jesus Christ, there is a process of formation available for the true disciple. Let me say it directly: The minister needs to decide to become formed by scripture, the church, and the Spirit. To enter this process is an act of the will in response to a Divine invitation.

Perhaps some warnings about the process are in order:

1. Beware of the tendency to try too hard, to depend on human ingenuity and effort to "achieve" spirituality.

2. Beware of entering into spiritual formation with the idea of earning ecclesiastical approval, or to curry favor with someone, or to meet some sort of institutional requirement.

3. Beware of entering into it with utilitarian objectives — the hope of becoming a "better," or "more successful" minister.

4. Beware of assuming that there are a series of steps to ascend, or a ladder to climb, that will assure the reaching of spiritual goals. There may, in fact, be some steps to take, and growth may be measurable. But for most pilgrims, the journey

will be marked by hills and valleys, detours and delays, failures and frustrations, with periodic breakthroughs and ecstasies.

5. Beware of undertaking the spiritual journey with any motivation or focus other than to praise God, and to honor the Lord of our lives.

Perhaps we need to make a distinction between spiritual *formation* and spiritual *transformation*. The former is partly a human enterprise — all that *we* do or refuse to do, think, or believe, to the end that life in Christ is furthered. Our Great Ally is the Holy Spirit. Transformation is mainly God's domain. It is through the bountiful provisions of the atonement that we can become new creations (2 Corinthians 5:17). It is God's mercy and grace, ultimately, that determines whether transformation takes place, or to what degree. So, spiritual formation might be said to be our feeble attempts to cooperate with the gracious initiatives of a loving God, to the end that we more nearly live our lives "in Christ."

In this chapter, I have identified some ways that spiritual formation will help us in the living of our lives; I have defined the terms; I have provided some theological, historical, and common sense foundations for the practice of spiritual formation. My invitation to you, then, is that you be especially attuned to your spiritual experiences as you read this book. I recommend a serious reading of spiritual theology (see, for example, works listed in the bibliography by Bloesch, Haughton, Leech, Lovelace, Nouwen and Underhill). Such intellectual and experiential openness will likely lead you to some significant new spiritual growth.

Testimony

For me, it was a delightful awakening when I slowly became aware that my walk with the Lord need not be an uptight, screwed down, perfectionistic, human effort to *do right*. Thankfully, I learned about grace! Really, I think I'm a better person now, a healthier, more effective minister, and I enjoy life more. I am learning to accept the process. I am learning to accept myself as human and fallible. I daily rely on grace, and I deeply believe God loves me, "just as I am." In fact, I may not be as "religious" as I once was, but I believe I'm more spiritual.

I am learning that it is "not I but Christ who lives in me" (Galatians 2:20), when it comes to living as a spiritual person. Life in Christ is not something I have achieved, rather it is a process, freely offered by the mercy of God. I'm learning that I don't have to *do* in order to gain His favor. He already loves me. On the contrary, I'm seeking to internalize and live out my belief that *I am* the glory of God. I was created in His image, and my task is to be true to my best (created) self.

How liberating it is to be freed from an oppressive theology that demands a "perfect performance" in this life! The spirit of spiritual formation, as I understand it, is that we are pilgrims on a journey. We are always struggling to become. Yet, paradoxically, I am more and more seeing spirituality in terms of "letting go and letting God." We struggle and do our part. But we also surrender to be shaped by God. This I am sure of: Process and relatedness form the ethos of spirituality. And the bottom line is grace!

II

Discipline

For the moment all discipline seems painful rather than pleasant; later it yields the peaceful fruit of righteousness to those who have been trained by it (Hebrews 12:11).

In beginning a consideration of spiritual discipline, we need to recognize three essential realities. First, God graciously gifts believers. Second, it matters how and what we think. Third, we need a game plan, if we are to grow in discipline.

Perhaps our greatest gift is potentiality. We have the created capacity to learn, grow, change, become. Beyond the innate capacity, there is a Divine summons that urges us onward. For each step of the journey the Holy Spirit is available to guide and stand beside us. Our efforts alone will not achieve discipline. We are gifted with potentiality.

It matters very much what we think, and how we think. Our mind-set shapes our decisions and commitments. God needs our cooperation, even our determination in this matter of discipline. So, we are faced with a challenge. Have we decided to pursue the deeper life? Are we open to the untried? Is our heart fixed on Jesus? What are our intentions?

39

Potentiality and determination are not enough. We need a plan. This brings us to the spiritual disciplines, which, combined with God's mercy and our efforts, enable us to move beyond surface living into the deeper life.

By spiritual disciplines, I mean everything that one intentionally and continuously seeks to do, or seeks not to do, under the direction of the Holy Spirit, to the end that one experiences more fully the life in Christ. *Discipline* is to intentionalize one's practice of the *disciplines*.

Believers generally feel called, in one way or another, to seek to change their world. That is a noble undertaking. There are multitudes of ministers committed to transforming their society in various and sundry ways. But we need to be reminded of the Divine call to *inner* transformation (Romans 12:1-2). Sadly, we ministers are often so busy preparing sermons, attending meetings, counseling with people, or planning strategy, that we just do not have the time (or take the time) needed for soul-renewal. We have been taught to serve God and the church. But in our zeal to serve God "out there," we fail to seek God "in here."

The disciplined inner life would, in my opinion, do much to dispel depression, prevent burnout, reduce tension and stress, and promote overall ministerial effectiveness. Most pastors have tried (or soon will try) working harder, getting more education, going to another workshop, devoting longer hours, and even using sincerity and charisma. Now, it may be time to try spiritual formation. When work is not working, try prayer!

I'm not suggesting that the spiritual disciplines are desperation parachutes, to be used when everything else has failed. Instead, spirituality is a style of life that undergirds and enables all the work that we do. Neither are the disciplines band-aids for the injuries of ministry. There are tremendous healing qualities in the spiritual disciplines, however.

The disciplines are, essentially, methods which we voluntarily employ to guide us in a life of holiness. Kenneth Jones' recent book is noteworthy because he takes the view that holiness is less a doctrine to be debated, or taught, or understood, and more a way of living in vital relationship with the Lord. Jones says,

> *To think of holiness as a set of rules to keep is to invite certain defeat. I invite you instead to think of holiness as a personal walk through life with a personal God. Holiness then is no longer memorizing a set of rules that seem unending. Holiness is following our living Lord by his grace and help ... Holiness then, is personal fellowship with a personal God (Jones, 1985, pp. 4-6).*

Not only is holiness a walk through life with a personal God, Jones also calls holiness an adventure. I like that! When I was younger, holiness often seemed like an oppressive, if not impossible, burden. But it liberates me to understand that, according to Jones:

> *Holiness is an adventure because it means going through life with God ... living under Gòd's direction, belonging only to God, being guided by the Holy Spirit, and learning from the God who made us (Jones, 1985, p. 4).*

That sounds like a journey or a pilgrimage. And in spiritual formation, the journey is our home! A *commitment* to holiness makes sense to me, and by God's grace, I can live that way. And so can you! The disciplines are part of God's graces that enable us to approach the fulfillment of God's plan for our lives, and to press toward the fulfillment of our own inner yearnings for life in Christ.

A List of Disciplines

I will now dare to offer a list of what I consider the essential spiritual disciplines, prepared from the perspective of Christian ministry. The spirit of the list is dynamic, not fixed. Persons considering it are invited to add to it, delete from it, or place emphasis wherever it seems appropriate to do so. Remember, the disciplines are what *we do*, in order to grow in Christ.

Richard Foster has done an excellent job of defining and describing the practice of Christian discipline. The first part of my list is a repetition of his list of spiritual disciplines.

I. The Inward Disciplines
    1. Meditation
    2. Prayer
    3. Fasting
    4. Study

II. The Outward Disciplines
    5. Simplicity
    6. Solitude
    7. Submission
    8. Service

III. The Corporate Disciplines
    9. Confession
    10. Worship
    11. Guidance
    12. Celebration

To Foster's list of twelve spiritual disciplines, I would like to add the nine "fruits of the Spirit" (Galatians 5:16-25), on the grounds that the purpose of the disciplines is to develop in us Christian character providing evidences of the Spirit of God. While it is true that the fruit are largely grace-gifts from God, it is also true that they are qualities of the Christian life which disciplined persons seek to develop by every means possible.

IV. The Character Disciplines
    13. Love
    14. Joy
    15. Peace
    16. Patience
    17. Kindness
    18. Goodness

19. Faithfulness
20. Gentleness
21. Self-control

Additionally, five other disciplines need to be added, especially when we consider the calling and the responsibilities of the Christian minister. To be effective, in my opinion, leaders need to be disciplined and spiritually formed in these areas:

V. The Ministry Disciplines
22. Witnessing
23. Caring
24. Visioning
25. Leading
26. Equipping

The temptation before me is to provide a detailed commentary on each of the twenty-six disciplines listed, and include definitions, biblical exegesis, suggestions for practice, and exhortations. But I shall resist! Rather, in this and subsequent chapters, I will provide a few practical ideas for the development and implementation of these disciplines in the life of the minister.

There are several other ministerial concerns which need some attention. While these may not be listed as disciplines (else the list gets out of hand), they surely do affect one's practice of all the spiritual disciplines. Let us now inquire into five significant ministerial problem areas (or opportunity areas!) — prioritizing, managing time, using leisure, keeping physically fit, and writing — which serve to support the development of discipline.

Priorities

The freedom to order one's priorities, is one of the meaningful fringe benefits of the minister. We can choose a lifestyle that enhances personal and spiritual growth, or we can choose work-habits and attitudes that wear away at the soul. So, the question becomes, what *are* our priorities?

Ministers make many choices and decisions. To distinguish between the peripheral and the central is a continuing challenge. Some of the toughest decisions we ever make is determining when to move ahead or when to stop or when to proceed cautiously. Occasionally, the light is clearly green or red. But more often, it seems to me, much of ministry is like proceeding under a caution light. That yellow light can be exceedingly subtle, and seductive, and deceptive. Sometimes it takes on the shades of green or red that I want to see in it, or that someone else tells me is there. And so I'm confused, and indecisive.

Nevertheless, despite the difficulties and the consequences, it is essential that we prioritize our roles. It is inappropriate for one person to prescribe a ready-made set of priorities for another person. But at the risk of being charged with doing so, here is a potential ordering of roles for the minister, to which I invite your reaction. By "role" I mean, a function, or a responsibility assigned to me by God, by myself, or by others.

Not one role on the following list is unimportant. In fact, I don't see how any one could be eliminated, and all are crucial to effective ministry. To "order" means to arrange according to some kind of ranking system. So, the items in the following list are arranged in the order of importance I place upon them. Taking the same list, how would you rearrange it to reflect your priorities? Are there any roles that need to be deleted from the list, or others added, in your opinion? You may want to spend some time with your journal before proceeding.

Ordering Role Priorities:
A Proposed Model for Professional Clergy

1. Believer
2. Spouse
3. Parent
4. Disciple

    5. Congregational Member
    6. Denominational Member
    7. Church Employee (Pastor)
    8. Community Participant
    9. World Citizen

Note that, according to this ordering, the minister's first priority is to respond in faith to the saving grace of Jesus Christ, and to live in Christ as an obedient believer. For those who are married, the second priority is to live in fidelity and love with one's spouse. (For an excellent discussion of commitment in marriage, and other pertinent topics, see Herbert and Fern Petersen, *Equality Marriage*, Revell, 1978). To discharge one's responsibilities as a father or mother takes precedence over pastoral or community obligations.

To be a disciple is to be a learner, living with concern and care for all of God's family, practicing a life of servanthood. Do you agree that this precedes being pastor of a congregation? The placement of Congregational Member suggests that one's membership in a local Body of Christ takes precedence over being a paid professional, or Church Employee. Not only is the pastor a member of the local congregation, but she/he values and nurtures a denominational connection. How important is it to you to be denominationally affiliated and fully cooperative?

An effective minister does not become so totally absorbed in his/her church-related work that there is no time left for involvement in the local community and the world community. Again, our world citizenship is not unimportant, but it behooves the pastor to be sure that she/he cares for the flock first (1 Peter 5:2; Acts 20:28).

Perhaps after reading this section and reflecting on it, you will take the time to do some writing in your journal. Are you open to reordering your priorities? Do you need to discuss some troublesome issues that have emerged with a trusted spiritual friend? Remember, if you pray about something, you need to be open for surprises, and perhaps to the need for some changes.

In addition to prioritizing one's ministerial roles, it is also essential to seek a balanced life-style. A wholistic view of life and ministry contributes to health and effectiveness. What are your life-priorities that help determine how your time, energy, and commitment will be apportioned and integrated?

The "priority pie" below, is an attempt to suggest some areas that need to be considered. The relative sizes of the "slices" will need to be determined by each person, after careful thought and prayer. One of the essential tasks in the process of spiritual formation is to constantly be at work ordering one's life-priorities in a spirit of discipline and flexibility.

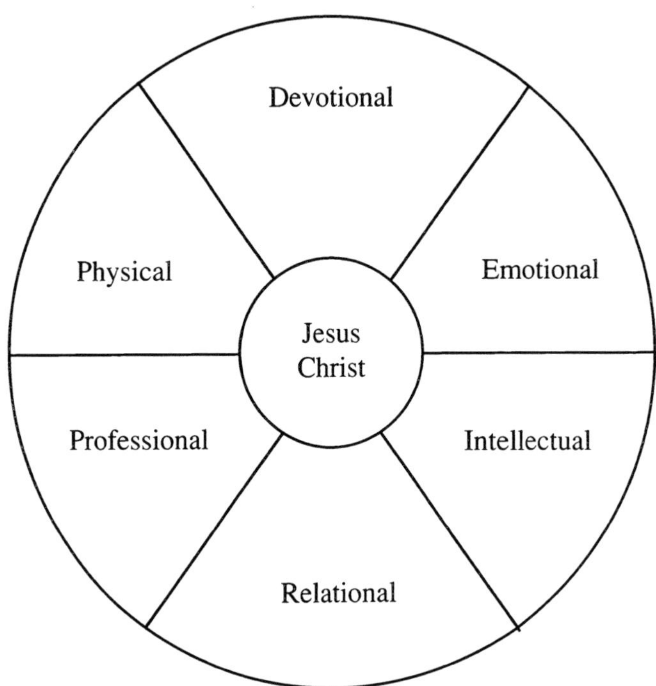

With Jesus Christ at the center, as a constant, how would you divide your "pie" at this point in your ministry? Your configuration can be revised for later situations and stages, of course, but which "slices" get most of your energy, time, and commitment now?

Time Management

The key to time management is management. It is essential to plan, to take charge, to live intentionally. Ministers like to be available, but to make oneself too available is likely to lead to feelings of being used or controlled. If we don't manage our time, others will, or circumstances will. Let me make a few suggestions to leaders about managing time.

First, prepare daily and weekly time schedules. On the samples provided, note that an effort has been made to organize the available time into blocks (see Appendix M). It helps to have a significant block of time to devote to a given task. In that way, one can often finish a job, instead of frantically running from task to task, constantly feeling interrupted, and seldom reaching closure on anything. Sound familiar?

The sample of the 17-Block Week (see Appendix M) provides a scheme for planning one's ideal work week. Of course, even though one carefully thinks through his/her schedules and priorities, and fills in all the blocks, such a design should be tentative. Ministers, of all people, never know what a week, or even a day, will hold. But to block out a week in this manner is an exercise in prioritizing.

Having used the 17-Block Week form to sketch in an ideal work week, one is then ready to use the Week at a Glance form (see Appendix M). Thus, the first form becomes something of a guide for the planning of a specific week. The Week at a Glance sheet then becomes an hour-by-hour, day-by-day schedule for the week. A fresh sheet is needed for each week of the year.

Personally, I have been using these forms for about ten years, and find that they provide a sense of direction, a helpful reminder, a bit of protection from intrusions, and a sense of accomplishment. Usually, I fill out a new Week at a Glance sheet early each Monday morning. On it I pencil in all known appointments, meetings, classes, spiritual formation time, family time and such like. I then place it in a prominent place on my desk. Students know they can stop in and sign up for an appointment, even when I'm not in my office. The secretary always knows my schedule. And I can stay pointed in the right direction, most of the time!

Second, learn to distinguish between what genuinely needs doing and what other people tell you needs doing. Many "emergencies" are not really emergencies at all. Generally speaking, the pastor should have a better sense of timing than does a troubled parishioner. Frequently, part of the solution to the problem, or part of the therapy itself, is for the parishioner to learn to wait. Of course, there are those occasions when a dedicated pastor will move heaven and earth to make personal contact with a needy person. The tricky part is being able to discern the reality of an emergency.

Third, reclaim some of the time normally spent in sermon preparation. In passing, let me observe that preaching, for the typical protestant pastor, is very time-consuming. I really believe that there are ways to do even more effective preaching, yet reduce the time needed for preparation, when the pastor prepares expository sermons and delivers them in a series format.

Fourth, help the congregation understand the time pressures of a pastor. Better understanding may result in more moderate expectations. Several years ago I made up a time study (see Appendix M) and used it in a congregation I served, in a Sunday evening service. I asked, "How much time does it take for a pastor to do an effective job?" I then announced that we would get the congregation's perception. So I divided the congregation into six groups of about twelve persons each. To each group I gave a sheet of paper containing one of the six categories (Appendix M). Each group was instructed to reach consensus on the amount of time they thought that a pastor needed each week in order to accomplish the tasks listed. After about 20 minutes, the groups returned to the sanctuary and we tallied the results. We eliminated section VI from the total and still came up with a 119-hour work-week. During the next three Sunday evenings we tried to discover more reasonable expectations!

Leisure

Recently, we've been nearly inundated by what has been written and spoken describing how busy and stressed most ministers are. Burnout is in vogue now. One fellow said he had been hearing about everybody burning out, so he decided to try it! Seriously, a word does need to be said about stress, and it needs to be said with urgency. Part of the urgency is, I think, that we Christian ministers generally have an inadequate theology of leisure.

The fact is, there is too much drivenness and compulsivity in the professional ministry and among the laity as well. There seem to be two contributing factors: The *pull* of needy persons and programs begging for leadership, and the *push* of a theology that requires us constantly to be **giving**. The result is tiredness, or ill health, or burnout. What can be done that will be preventive and healing?

Perhaps the first thing we need to do is to read the internal signs that may be alerting us to problems. Some of the more obvious signs of stress, which indicate that a person may be on a burnout track, are the following:

1. General fatigue, which rest doesn't seem to cure.
2. Frequent headaches.
3. Inability to get to sleep, or waking too early.
4. Feelings or expressions of frustration or anger.
5. Unusually rigid, stubborn, or determined.
6. Negative, critical, or sarcastic feelings and expressions.
7. Elevated blood pressure.
8. Nervous, edgy, hyper-active.
9. Depression.

When blips such as the above begin to show up on our physical/emotional/spiritual screens, this is no time for denial, or for some kind of ego-driven display of virility. Some people can work 70 hours a week, seldom take a day off, be very productive in their efforts, and enjoy it all. Fine. But these persons need to be fully in touch with themselves, and very sure that some of these blips *aren't* there. It is possible to be so busy and so stressed that one cannot see the blips. It is then, especially, that a good spiritual friend or supervisor could be of tremendous help.

In addition, one needs to understand and accept one's own biorhythms. Some of us were built for speed, others for economy, others for productivity, others for strength — and maybe some for comfort. The point is, we need to know if we really are suited for the fast lane, or whether another lane might be healthier for us. Some of us are early risers and some of us are late sleepers. Some people can function on five hours of sleep, others require nine. It is important to accept our unique biological clock rather than comparing ourselves to others and then feeling cheated or guilty. Of course, some minor changes in our biorhythms do occur, especially as we pass through the various stages of life and ministry, or if we work at effecting change, or when circumstances demand that we make changes.

How well do you know yourself, your heart rate, your blood pressure, your cholesterol level, your blood count, and so on? And do you listen to the people nearest you — your spouse, your physician, your ecclesiastical superior, your spiritual friend? What are they trying to tell you, or what would they tell you if you asked and really listened? I am not inviting you to adopt a fearful, guarded, hypochondriacal approach to life. But I am inviting you to know yourself. Are you reading the signs?

A second thing we might need to do is to change our attitude toward leisure. For many of us in ministry, our theology supports a workaholic lifestyle. Granted, good biblical theology doesn't drive us, but *our* theology may. And our theology is, typically, a blend of our personality, the influence of our models, our own expectations and our perception of the expectations of others, along with our personal interpretations of Scripture. (As you can see, I'm thinking more in terms of applied theology.)

So, what may be needed is theological permission to change our attitude toward leisure and begin to view rest, relaxation, and retreat, more positively. We may need to move beyond those adolescent impressions, commitments, and early work habits that were shaped by "Work for the Night is Coming" and "Every Hour for Jesus" (songs from my heritage), sermons on "go make disciples" and "be ye therefore perfect," and an inner urge to be totally involved. The basic meanings of those messages are good, of course. But being very serious, dedicated persons, we took the messages too literally. And while the tapes are still playing in our head and heart, some of us have found that, with the passing of years, our body is not able to bear the weight of youthful commitments and work patterns. Do you know anyone like that?

If this description is accurate for many or even for some ministers, what can be done? If it is true that there is an extensive fellowship of ministerial workaholics who unwittingly abide by a works-righteousness theology and are motivated by perfectionistic tendencies and personality type, what is the way out of the dilemma?

Perhaps a thorough Bible study on rest, relaxation, retreat, and leisure, would be a good place to begin. Special attention should be given to the times when Jesus went apart to pray, and when He called His disciples into the mountains or to the lake in order to find some rest and peace. Jesus needed these times of vacation, and so do we.

Maybe a few good sermons would help. For starters listen to some sermons, and even dare to preach on themes such as tarrying, resting, solitude, enabling, peace, and quiet. We've probably heard enough sermons urging persons to go, do, work, strive, contend, and try harder. Are you ready to say to yourself and others, "Relax, God loves you? Don't try so hard to get God to like you. He does!"

You also might want to consider cutting back on church

activities, instead of adding others. I am not advising retrench-ment. I am advising evaluation. Is *this* activity essential to our mission? Does *this* activity really need my involvement, or is it my ego that needs the involvement?

Finally, in answer to the question, "What can I do?" my suggestion is, take some time off. Go ahead and do it! Don't wait for somebody else to arrange it. Are you in charge of your schedule? Begin with a simple vacation of a week or two that includes your family if you are married. Then schedule a series of two- or three-day prayer retreats, preferably in a quiet, con-templative setting (see Appendix F for a directory of such retreat centers). As an economical alternative, consider camping or using a trailer or motor home, as a means of getting away from the routine. A long-term goal might be a sabbatical leave of several months (see Appendix O). Does "alone with God" sound like a good idea to you?

Physical Fitness

There might be a few persons here and there who object to any mention of diet, exercise, and weight control in a book about spirituality and ministry. I trust that I will be able to say what needs to be said with compassion and gentleness.

Here is a word of truth: Spiritual health is total health. Wholistic is the word! To be undisciplined in one area of life and ministry is to be affected in all areas. Thus, on the grounds of "wholth" (wholistic health) and balance and common sense, I appeal to you, be disciplined in your eating and exercising habits. Don't carry that extra weight around. It does not glorify God, nor is it a good Christian witness.

Let me make some simple, practical, and economical suggestions that, if followed, might help you to keep physi-cally fit.

1. Reduce your salt and sugar intake. The harm they do the human body has been well documented, and it is surprising

how good food or beverages taste without them, once our taste buds get adjusted.

2. Discipline yourself to cut down on certain foods — starches, sweets, snacks, and second helpings.

3. Drink a lot of water. It is usually inexpensive, and the body needs it.

4. Eat plenty of roughage, such as uncooked fruit and vegetables (including the peelings!), and bran in various forms.

5. Walk more and ride less. Walking just may be the most complete exercise. It can be done when dressed to go to a meeting, and it can be carried over into old age. Avoid elevators. Park the car and walk.

Writing

One other area which serves to support the development of the spiritual disciplines is writing. At first glance, writing seems to introduce a dissonant element into our discussion of discipline. We've been exhorted to "read, read, read," and we are aware of how reading contributes to spirituality. Now, I'd like to exhort us to "write, write, write." Perhaps its contribution to spirituality is less well documented.

I think writing is an important and necessary activity for the minister. It should become part of one's daily discipline, with an occasional larger part of a day given more fully to it. What sort of writing would contribute to the spiritual formation of the minister?

Sermons, may be written. The preacher who writes will be clearer, more forceful, more logical, more effective. To write a sermon in full is to provide a permanent record of what was intended, and it provides an opportunity for revision and growth in communication skills. This is not to argue on behalf of delivery from a manuscript, but even an extemporaneous delivery is enhanced by the discipline of writing the sermon.

Public prayers may written. Personally, I prefer to deliver pastoral prayers extemporaneously, but that preference calls all the more for preparation. The writing helps with content, vocabulary, structure, and emotion. Thus, with the full prayer written out, one can pray extemporaneously (or with very limited notes) from the pulpit in an appropriate, confident, effective manner.

Creative writing may be done periodically by the minister. What I mean is that she/he should create some poetry, fiction, short stories, biographies, humorous accounts, descriptions, dialogues, anecdotes, plays, articles, and such like. Of course you can do it. I heard that objection! A creative diversion of this sort might help provide a spark of lightness and healing and playfulness.

Personal journals may be written. Journal-keeping is therapeutic and growth-enhancing. Brief entries each day, or most days, provide a record of feelings, insights, movings of the Spirit, events, hopes, prayers, and more. On some days, a simple notation of an event is all that seems to be needed. On other days, deep emotions and heart-hungers pour forth, page after page. I like to write personal prayers, and keep a record of what I'm praying about. A journal should reflect personal needs, hopes, and victories, not the conformity to some idealized patterns. Perhaps the bottom line is that a *daily* journal is a visible reminder of a commitment to seek God's presence in a humble, patient, open manner.

Finally, just in case this exhortation to write needs to be defended, let me summarize by identifying a few reasons why I think that the minister who would be effective needs to write.

1. Writing produces clarity. When one writes, there is pressure to express it simply, directly, clearly. Furthermore, writing helps one to think and to speak more clearly.

2. Writing produces insight. To write well, one often has to check information or understanding, and research the subject. Thus, knowledge is increased.

3. Writing produces growth. To be exposed to new ideas, new challenges, new experiences, and then write about them, inevitably produces change and growth in the writer.

4. Writing produces wholeness. Frequently, writing is therapeutic. The flow of thoughts, feelings, and insights, results in cleansing and release. I really believe that writing on a regular basis contributes to mental and spiritual health. To ingest human contacts, books, and other stimuli, but to do no writing (reflection, integration, expression), may result in a sort of generalized intellectual, emotional, and spiritual constipation. There is a basic human need to release, to give out, to be heard, and putting words onto paper is one way of doing this.

5. Writing produces fulfillment. There is a sense in which the process of writing is, of itself, fulfilling. To be able to put words together in such a way as to convey a message, is rewarding. Beyond that, there is the satisfaction of anticipating or knowing that what is written will influence others. Try writing! It just may produce some positive benefits in your spiritual development.

Conclusion

In this Chapter, I have tried to say that the spiritual disciplines are means or methods which we employ in a committed fashion, to enable us to live holy lives. A list of twenty-six disciplines was provided. Some other contributors to discipline (prioritizing, managing time, using leisure, keeping physically fit, writing) were added because of their significance to ministry.

I read a story several years ago in the *Taylor University Magazine*, of a man who built his own small boat, then sailed it alone across the Pacific Ocean. He landed safely in Australia, after weeks of loneliness, deprivation, and fear. He then flew back to California, a hero. An interviewer asked him, "What were you thinking about when you were out there in the middle of the ocean, alone, and you knew a storm was about to hit?" His answer went something like this: "I was hoping that I had not built my boat too quickly, or too cheaply, or too carelessly. While I was building it, I was anxious to finish it so I could get on with my voyage. I detested the hours of labor in preparation for the trip, so I hurried the building of the boat. But out there in the ocean, I was hoping that I had done an adequate job, and wishing that I had built the boat even more carefully.''

Ministerial preparation is somewhat like that. Most of us are in a hurry to get on with ministry. The spiritual disciplines remind us that we are always in preparation. We will spend the bulk of our lives getting ready. The best preparation for ministry is living, and the best education comes from life.

The only appropriate thing to do with life is to live it, a day at a time. So, why the hurry to get on to someplace else? The Bible says, "They that wait for the Lord shall renew their strength" (Isaiah 40:31). There is that word wait again! The journey is our home, so the time spent in preparation or getting acquainted with the disciplines is essential and should not be hurried.

It would be unfortunate indeed to get out into the middle of our ministry only to discover that we had failed to prepare adequately. That discovery might be disastrous for us, as well as for those who look to us for the care of their souls. The spiritual disciplines provide paths to preparation at the deepest levels.

Here is a sentence that I hope grabs you: *The dignity of a vocation is always to be measured by the seriousness of the preparation made for it.*

We are heirs of the King, doing Kingdom business! You talk about a position with dignity. There is no more noble undertaking than that of becoming prepared servants to the King and the kingdom. If, then, Christian ministry is a high calling, how important is preparation for it? How willing are you to be educated, trained, and spiritually formed?

How do you answer people who ask, "Why are you spending all that time in college, or seminary, or program of study, or prayer, or Bible study, or spiritual retreats, or workshops, and so on?" The inference is why don't you get out and get on with the work, in the real world? And sometimes you feel that they may be right, don't you?

But your determination and commitment to be a disciplined minister of Jesus Christ keep you going in your preparation to serve, in obedience to your calling. Effective ministry requires preparation. Discipline (including practicing the disciplines) is the "stuff" that the Holy Spirit can use to enable ministers to minister.

III

Direction

Give thy servant therefore an understanding mind . . .
that I may discern between good and evil . . . (1 Kings
3:9).

In Chapter I, I gave a list of what I consider to be the seven basic components of spiritual formation (inner hunger, communal worship, private devotions, reading and study, spiritual direction, social involvement, and humility). The fifth component, direction, is the subject of this chapter. Our first task, then, is to provide a working definition of spiritual direction, keeping in mind that direction is only one part of formation.

According to Sandra Schneiders, spiritual direction may be defined as,

> *A process carried out in the context of a one-to-one relationship in which a competent guide helps a fellow Christian in the spiritual life by means of personal encounters that have the directee's spiritual growth as their explicit object (Culligan, ed., 1983, p. 46).*

Barry and Connolly provide this definition:

59

> *We define Christian spiritual direction, then, as help given
> by one Christian to another which enables that person
> to pay attention to God's personal communication to him
> or her, to respond to this personally communicating God,
> to grow in intimacy with this God, and to live out the
> consequences of the relationship (Barry and Connolly,
> 1982, p. 8).*

A definition which suggests some helpful but potentially troublesome parallels, is the one provided by Kevin Culligan:

> *Spiritual direction is a counseling ministry in the church
> which helps Christians draw closer to God, especially
> through prayer (Culligan, ed., 1983, p. 9).*

The problem, as I see it, with linking direction to counseling, is the complex variety of philosophies and practices of counseling. To use the word "counseling," then, may add more confusion than clarity to the definition.

These next three definitions are mine, with thanks for a lot of help from my friends and companions along the way:

> *Spiritual direction is a process in which one person guides
> another, or others, in reflecting on their experiences with
> God, in light of their unique calling, and in obedience
> to the Word of God.*

> *A spiritual director is a person, who, at my invitation
> monitors my spiritual development.*

> *A spiritual director is a spiritual mentor.*

With these sketchy definitions as a beginning point, let us now paint a larger picture of spiritual direction. Note that, "director" is being used interchangeably with guide, companion, spiritual friend, soul friend, mentor, confessor, or spiritual counselor, though each has subtle nuances that provide different emphases.

Perhaps the first question that faces us is this: Can spiritual direction be defended as valid for our generation? I believe the answer is yes, for several good reasons.

Why Spiritual Direction?

First, there are good *theological* reasons for the practice of spiritual direction. High on God's scale of priorities are the concepts of community, congregation, and covenant. It is His good will that the concepts become reality. But to function as Christian individuals, in community, as part of a congregation, living covenant-lives, is no easy matter. It does not occur naturally. It takes the grace of God, and some person-to-person nurture for the life in Christ to become real. To the degree that our personal relationship with God is vital, community, congregation, and covenant will become real.

Theology must move beyond doctrine, catechism, lectures, and facts, if it is to serve its true function. Ultimately, the function of theology is to lead to experience — a vital encounter with a personal God, with other persons in the human family, and with the whole creation.

Spiritual direction adds the relational dimension to the doctrinal and transcendent elements of the Christian faith. It is obvious that not all of God's holy will and divine provisions have been written in books, nor could we learn them fully by reading. Revelation is continuous and creative. Codification and memorization of doctrinal principles will not necessarily produce true disciples. In the process of faith development, life-giving relationships give vitality to the community, the congregation, and the covenant.

The faith is best passed on in the manner Jesus used. He called persons (learners) to be *with* Him (Mark 3:13-14). After engaging with them in an intensive spiritual direction relationship, He sent them forth. When they returned, periodically, the direction continued (see Mark 6:30-32). This period of preparation had cognitive or educational aspects for the disciples, to be sure, but it was also intensely relational.

To have a spiritual director is to add the dimension of heart to the process of Christian growth that is often very heady (classes, study, information). Ideally, of course, a wise spiritual director will not engage in any artificial or superficial dichotomizing of the two. True spirituality is a blend of the heart and the head, as one lives a holistic life in Christ. And theology at its best promotes wholeness.

Second, there are good *social-psychological* reasons for the practice of spiritual direction. The human race was created to live in community. We really were never intended to live as islands of self-sufficiency. At a deep level, we need the camaraderie, fellowship, support, and mutual stimulation that family and community affords. We also need the confrontation, correction, and guidance that community provides. Sometimes, community at its best functions as sand paper to painfully and patiently shape us up. Spiritual direction may not always be enjoyable!

One of the basic human needs is to love and to be loved. Another very basic need is to speak and to be spoken to. We need to hear from others and we need to sense that we are heard by others. I am convinced that it is not so much what we don't know that cripples us emotionally as it is what we can't talk about. It is essential for the person on spiritual pilgrimage to find ways to experience self-disclosure or self-expression. An experience with God cannot be kept inside, else it dies!

Scott Walker quotes from *The Meaning of Persons*, by Paul Tournier, who says,

> *We become fully conscious only of what we are able to express to someone else. We may already have had a certain inner intuition about it, but it must remain vague so long as it is unformulated (Walker, 1985, p. 154).*

Third, there are good *historical-traditional* reasons for the practice of spiritual direction. Or, put another way, history and tradition have validated the use of spiritual direction as an appropriate means of spiritual formation.

Christian spiritual direction has been practiced in one form or another in the church since the post-Apostolic era. According to Leech,

The first sign of spiritual direction within the Christian tradition on any sizeable scale can be seen in the Desert Fathers in Egypt, Syria, and Palestine in the fourth and fifth centuries. Disciples would seek out the advice and guidance of these holy men of the desert (Leech, 1977, p. 41).

Some of the early notable teachers, writers, and practitioners of spiritual direction were Antony (c. 251-356), Jerome (340-420), Augustine (354-430), Evagrius Ponticus (345-399), John Cassian (360-435), Gregory (540-604), and Alcuin (735-804). Medieval writers include Bernard of Clairvaux (1090-1153), Francis of Assisi (1181-1226), Meister Eckhart (1260-1327), Johann Tauler (1300-1361), and John Ruysbroeck (1293-1381). Later notable writers, from whom we can learn about direction, include Teresa of Avila (1515-1582), John of the Cross (1542-1591), Jacob Boehme (1575-1624), Brother Lawrence (c. 1605-1691), Blaise Pascal (1623-1662), George Fox (1624-1691), John Woolman (1720-1772), Evelyn Underhill (1875-1941), and Thomas Merton (1915-1968).

A mere listing of names by itself is not very convincing to be sure. But if one would take the time to read about the spiritual lives of these great saints, one would be impressed with the emphasis each placed upon the importance of seeking after God, engaging in the search with another person who can offer support, encouragement, and guidance.

For further reading in the historical development of spiritual direction, refer to the books listed in the bibliography by Bouyer, Cox, Holmes, Leech, Underhill, and Wakefield. In addition, some specialized libraries may have available in the reference section such works as *Ancient Christian Writers, Classics of Western Spirituality, Library of Christian Classics,* and *Nicene and Post-Nicene Fathers*, all multi-volume sets. Two recent and less intimidating books on the practice of Christian spirituality (growth in holiness) are:

Alexander, Donald L. (ed.). **Christian Spirituality: Five Views of Sanctification** (Intervarsity Press, 1988). The contributors came from a Reformed, Lutheran, Wesleyan, Pentecostal and Contemplative perspective.

Mass, Robin and Gabriel O'Donnell (eds.). **Spiritual Traditions for the Contemporary Church** (Abingdon, 1990). This is a textbook which covers the field in an introductory way.

Let us turn now to a brief examination of post Reformation Protestant practices of spiritual direction. Most of the early Protestant reformers were concerned in one way or another about the issue of sacerdotalism, which includes the notion that Christians are obligated to approach God through an intermediary, usually a priest. In the opinion of most early Protestants, the Catholic Church hierarchy had inserted itself as the mediator between God and humankind.

While the priesthood of all believers is an idea whose time had come, there was a certain amount of fallout associated with it. For example, the priesthood of believers idea was used by some persons and groups to exalt individualism or private piety. Others interpreted it in such a way as to minimize community and covenant commitments, and promoted a highly personalized salvation, a casual approach to the institutional church, and a cavalier mentality with regard to ministry.

Once the principle had been established that believers could break away from the main body of Christians without impunity, then the seeds for future discord and division had been sown. Protestants and Catholics alike have continued to separate and form new church groups. Furthermore, an individualistic style of ministry and clergy leadership became all too common in some, if not all, Protestant groups.

Now and again during the history of Protestantism, and even in recent times, congregations have perpetuated the sad practice of dividing on the pretext of doctrinal purity or biblical integrity. This attitude of ''I'll change churches,'' or ''I'll start another church,'' diminishes Christian fellowship, cooperation, mutual support, and mutual accountability, it seems to me. Of course, someone had to be courageous enough to create schism, or there never would have been a Protestant Reformation! But my point is, we need to be able to face up to the positive as well as the negative aspects.

So, for reasons, some of which go back to the Protestant Reformation, spiritual direction never did become very popular among Protestants, nor is it now. But through the years, there has been a modest number of persons who taught and practiced it. According to Leech, Luther exercised a ministry of personal direction, as did Calvin, Bucer, Spener, Richard Baxter, George Fox, John Wesley, Dietrich Bonhoeffer, and others (Leech, 1977, pp. 84-88).

In addition to the Reformation influences that seemed to discourage the practice of spiritual direction in the Protestant churches, it is also apparent that the Puritan ethic of strong independence (for example, consider Bunyan's Christian who struggles *alone* against great difficulties, but with *personal* access to God), the American ideals of free enterprise and frontier, plus the competitive, success-oriented atmosphere typical in the United States, have all worked together to denigrate the work of spiritual direction. The popular myth is that psychotherapy is for those who aren't tough enough to make it alone (the ideal). Somewhat the same myth pervades the spiritual realm, so that ideally, one turns to God privately and help is received. But to share a spiritual need with another person, or to seek a spiritual guide — this is a sure sign of weakness, or failure, or immaturity. And our ego can't handle that inference!

Zwingli generally gets the credit for rejecting auricular confession, and the Protestant reformers generally followed his lead. According to Leech, who quotes from McNeill, *A History of the Cure of Souls*, Zwingli said,

> *Auricular confession is nothing but a consultation in which we receive from him whom God has appointed . . . advice as to how we can secure peace of mind (Leech, 1977, p., 85).*

Interestingly, however, the Protestant reformers and their

followers not only rejected the use of the confessional booth, but also tended to reject any form of spiritual guidance, or pastoral counseling. They took the path, instead, of establishing a private relationship with God, and no human being would be permitted to intrude, or in some cases, even assist. Important exceptions to this generalization would be the practice among Quakers of what was called mutual admonition. Also, the Mennonites and Brethren groups that practiced various forms of shunning and banns did so for the care and cure of souls. The Wesleyan Class Meetings featured an examination of conscience, accountability to the group, mutual sharing, and prayer. But none of these have been widely practiced by 20th century evangelical Christians.

In passing, perhaps it needs to be said that pastoral counseling has seen a remarkable growth in this century, especially among what might be broadly referred to as the more liberal denominations. Pastoral counseling seems to be less popular among the more conservative groups, which remain the bastion of private piety. Furthermore, the pastoral counseling that *is* done these days more often flies under the flag of psychology and psychotherapy, than under the flag of theology and righteous admonition (1 Thessalonians 5:14 and Matthew 18:15-18).

In recent times (particularly in the United States since the early 1900s) there has been an emphasis among Protestants on righteous works, social reform, Christian action, and liberation theology, and less focus upon introspection, contemplation, spiritual retreats, and prayer. I was a student in seminary during the sixties, and the mood then was, "We're too busy changing our world to pray. Let those who have nothing else to do, pray!"

Times have changed, however. Barry and Connolly, in the Preface of their book, have this to say:

> *During the last ten years spiritual direction has gained a surprising currency in Christian circles. Many more people, both Protestant and Roman Catholic, know about*

Fourth, and finally, there are some good *biblical* reasons
for the practice of spiritual direction. In fact, some of our most
useful models are from Scripture. Let us now examine several
examples, none of which provides a fully developed model for
spiritual direction, but when considered together, patterns and
principles emerge which suggest guidelines for this ministry.

A New Testament Model

Jesus provided an example of spiritual formation, broadly defined, and He also engaged in a more specific spiritual
direction relationship, particularly with His disciples. When
He called His disciples "to be with him" (Mark 3:13-14), and
they responded positively, the first Christian spiritual direction relationship was begun.

Here are some verses selected from Mark 1, 3, 6, and 9,
that give us some feel for how Jesus used spiritual direction
to help prepare His disciples.

*And in the morning, a great while before day, he rose
and went out to a lonely place, and there he prayed. And
Simon and those who were with him, followed him, and
they found him and said to him, 'everyone is searching
for you' . . . And he went up into the hills and called to
him those whom he desired; and they came to him. And
he appointed twelve to be with him, and to be sent out
to preach and have authority . . . Then Jesus went home
. . . The Apostles returned to Jesus, and told him all that
they had done and taught. And he said to them, 'Come
away by yourselves to a lonely place, and rest awhile.'
For many were coming and going, and they had no leisure
even to eat . . . and when he had entered the house, his
disciples asked him privately, 'Why could we not cast out
(the unclean spirit)?' And he said to them, 'this kind cannot be driven out by anything but prayer.'*

From these Scriptures, we may infer some features of Jesus' way of doing spiritual direction (or mentoring), from the perspective of the ones being directed.

1. The Disciples had a Mentor (director) who modeled spiritual disciplines ("he went to a lonely place, and there he prayed").

2. The Disciples sought out their Mentor ("they found Him").

3. The Disciples learned the importance of the lonely place.

4. The Disciples experienced a sense of calling (Jesus "called to him those whom he desired").

5. The Disciples understood that their appointment was "to be with him."

6. The Disciples were delegated and set free to serve ("sent out to preach and have authority . . . Then Jesus went home").

7. The Disciples returned for supervision, learning, and support ("The Apostles returned to Jesus and told him all that they had done and taught").

8. The Disciples benefited from their Mentor's concern and care for them ("come away by yourselves to a lonely place, and rest awhile").

9. The Disciples experienced the rhythm of work and rest.

10. The Disciples learned that prayer was necessary in order for them to be effective ("driven out by prayer").

Of course, it may be argued that these verses outline the archetypal pastoral supervision relationship, or the model for all subsequent field education, or the description of a lay training program. And I would agree. But my point is, that early in their preparation, the Disciples were confronted with the importance of prayer, and the need for companionship in ministry. It is a theme that runs through the life and ministry of Jesus from beginning to end (see Mark 14:32-42). And it will be a part of the fabric of our ministries when we truly learn our lessons from our Chief Mentor.

A question that often haunts me is this: Do I engage in any prayer-driven ministries? Is there *anything* that I do for God's sake, which depends upon prayer and the guidance and power of the Holy Spirit? Or, is my ministry ego-driven, or fear of failure-driven? Have I accomplished anything lately by the power of prayer? I hope you are asking yourself those questions, too.

An Old Testament Model

We have looked at one New Testament passage, now let us consider one Old Testament passage which might contain some clues for an understanding of spiritual direction. 1 Samuel 3:1-21, contains the story of Eli and Samuel (director and directee, respectively) and how they mutually discerned the will of God for both of them. Notice the following characteristics of spiritual direction as exemplified in the relationship of Eli and Samuel:

1. Samuel was under Eli's direction (v. 1).
2. Eli helped Samuel discern the voice of God (vv. 8-9).
3. Eli instructed Samuel to pay attention to the voice of God (v. 8-9).
4. Eli helped Samuel exercise patience in hearing and obeying God (v. 5-9).
5. Eli insisted that Samuel obey God, even though he was fearful to do so (v. 17).
6. Samuel grew and developed under Eli's direction (v. 19).
7. Samuel became established as a Prophet of God (v. 20-21).

There are other human relationships described in the Bible which illustrate the directing or mentoring process, and the good which is derived from it. One might find a study of Elijah/Elisha, Daniel/Solomon, Paul/Timothy, and other such relationships, very enlightening and inspiring. But let us keep in mind that, while mentoring or coaching one another in faith development is a time-honored and useful enterprise, the Chief Shepherd of our souls is our Lord, Jesus Christ. We find great benefit in having a director to guide our encounters with God. But the director must not become a God-substitute, nor a guru, but a spiritual director simply directs the *process* by which encounters with God occur.

Terminology

Perhaps it would be helpful at this point to deal with certain objections to the use of the word "direction." I have chosen to write about spiritual direction because the term has dimensions of richness and traditional use that are not found in any of its alternatives. Undoubtedly, it communicates more clearly to more people than do terms like spiritual companion or spiritual counselor. However, it is important to remember that direction refers more to the process than to the persons.

I am keenly aware, though, that direction and director have some negative connotations these days. For those persons who reached adolescence during the forties or fifties or before, the objections might not be as great. Those in that age bracket learned quite naturally and painlessly to respect their elders, to accept the authority of teachers, parents, and pastors, and to seek from them such guidance and help that were needed to negotiate adolescence. Such was not the case for those who reached adolescence in the sixties and seventies. That was the generation which discovered that everyone over 30 was hopelessly outdated and unreliable! So, persons in that age bracket may sincerely be troubled with the notion of being "under" spiritual direction. And to be honest, when it is understood that way, I don't like that sort of "direction" myself!

So now we are in the nineties, having been bombarded by and deeply changed by ideas about the uniqueness and value of the individual, personal autonomy and creativity, and so on. Humanism really has gotten to us, with both positive and negative results!

Now that our anthropological and theological formulations are being cast in a slightly different vocabulary (thankfully), perhaps it *is* time to substitute another term for "spiritual direction." With its vestiges of authoritarianism, ecclesiastical control or manipulation, and obedient submission, perhaps a different term *would* encourage a more positive response, especially among younger Christians.

Still, spiritual direction is a perfectly acceptable term when we realize that the direction has less to do with persons (telling, requiring), and more to do with the process (listening, inquiring, waiting, praying), to the end that the directee becomes more self-motivated and oriented toward growth.

I think that the word "mentor," or better, "spiritual mentor," has a lot going for it. Mentoring is widely understood and used in business, industry, and education. For further reading in this area, let me suggest two books: *You and Your Network*, by Fred Smith, and *The Fire in Their Eyes: Spiritual Mentors for the Christian Life*, by Gregory M. Smith.

Spiritual Friends

Personally, I prefer, and am now using more frequently than any other, the term "spiritual friend." It seems to assist us in getting away from some of the managerial or inferior-superior connotations inherent in the general understanding of "direction." It moves us, I think, more toward the idea of an egalitarian relationship.

I would now like to describe a seminary program which we call Spiritual Friends. I have been a member of the faculty at the School of Theology, Anderson University (Anderson, Indiana), since September 1978. In 1983, I gladly accepted appointment as Director of Spiritual Life for the Seminary. This gave me an opportunity to do something specific about a long-standing concern of mine, namely, that students in ministerial preparation should develop a disciplined approach to the deeper life, to go along with their acquisition of knowledge and skills for ministry.

For nearly a year, I read, wrote letters, attended seminars, and talked to people (along with my regular duties), in order to prepare myself for the assignment. In the Fall of 1984, I distributed to the Seminary community a brief paper on spiritual formation and seminary education, and presented the idea of Spiritual Friends. I also began contacting a group of people in the Anderson area who, it seemed to me, were on a spiritual pilgrimage, and who, I believed might have an interest in working with students on a spiritual level. Within a few months, I had identified about forty persons who agreed to explore with me the possibilities in this proposed new program. About thirty of them actually did some reading that I suggested and attended orientation sessions.

These Spiritual Friends were certainly not professional spiritual directors. Rather, they were secretaries, teachers, church agency executives, pastors, homemakers, and so on. A significant number of them were retired persons. They did not claim to be great saints. They were not therapists. They simply made themselves available to engage with a seminary student for one semester, in an attempt to make their life in Christ more real for both of them.

During that first year, the group was given a basic introduction to spiritual direction by means of personal conversations with me, by guided reading, and by group instruction. (This process continues as new Friends are added to the program, and others drop out for one reason or another.) Since what we were attempting to do was not part of the tradition of our faith group, we all struggled together, without benefit of experience. And we are still struggling and learning!

I sought to lead the group of Spiritual Friends to certain basic understandings, and to relate skills which they already possessed to this new endeavor. What follows is a condensation of the "curriculum" that we used in those early sessions.

Most of us, at one time or another, have experienced the warmth and support of a caring, praying, encouraging friend, pastor, or relative. God seems to gift some people with empathy, and we gladly turn to them. All of us can develop our gifts and skills in this area, and make ourselves more available to persons who are aware of spiritual needs. All sincere Christians desire to invest a bit of themselves in the developing lives of others.

One group of spiritually receptive persons in the Anderson community is the student body at the School of Theology. These students literally come from around the world. They come in a variety of ages, races, and personality types — but they all have spiritual needs and strong desires to grow as persons and as ministers. Many of them are looking for a friend, a confidant, someone to listen, someone to care about them, someone to pray with them. Not all students need such a person, of course, but many do.

Seminary can be a lonely, discouraging, disturbing, tiring experience. Most students do not have a support system immediately available to them. They left that, and much more, back home. So they are looking for a relationship that might help them get adjusted in Anderson, get comfortable in their academic pursuits, and maintain a closeness with God that will undergrid this new adventure.

Spiritual Friends are:

1. *Mentors of the devotional life.*
2. *Fellow-pilgrims on the spiritual journey.*
3. *Guides who walk with us through struggles.*
4. *Teachers who listen, evaluate, and study with us.*
5. *Witnesses who share what God is doing in their lives.*
6. *Directors who guide us to resources, urge us, and confront us patiently.*
7. *Creators who inspire in us the will to go on, and the courage to wait.*

Spiritual Friends are Not:

1. *Super saints.*
2. *Persons who will do the praying for another.*
3. *Givers of quick, easy answers.*
4. *Dispensers of advice.*

5. Psychotherapists or counselors.
6. Convenient "dumping" places.
7. Managers of another's spiritual life.

Who, then, is a Spiritual Friend? A Spiritual Friend is a faithful, growing Christian who covenants to enter into a process with another person in which the latter will reflect on his/her own experience with God, in light of a unique calling, and in obedience to the Word of God.

The Spiritual Friend is not a model, in the sense that a model is expected to have achieved perfection, and thus worthy of being imitated. But Spiritual Friends are mentors who facilitate a process of spiritual growth by enabling, as best they can, that relationship that already exists between the student and God.

The Spiritual Friend is available to assist the student upon the student's initiation, but the Friend does not assume responsibility for the student's spiritual life. Their meetings always focus on the deeper life, not so much on intellectual issues, nor problems of everyday living.

Persons who become Spiritual Friends to School of Theology students are expected to do some specialized reading and attend orientation sessions led by the Director of Spiritual Life. Students and Friends are "matched" by the Director, upon the student's application to the Program, and the student initiates the relationship with the Friend. Generally, the two get together for an hour every two or three weeks (sometimes more frequently), and the student makes herself/himself accountable to the Friend in very specific ways in order to grow in the Spiritual disciplines.

In order to help you understand the basic idea of being a spiritual friend to another, I have given a brief summary of the philosophy and practice of the Spiritual Friends Program at the School of Theology. This material was first shared with the persons in Anderson who expressed an interest in participating in the Program in the fall of 1984.

By the fall of 1985, I was ready to present the Program to the student body. What follows is an outline of the material that was shared with the incoming class at orientation sessions and in other settings. Our goal was that all students be made aware of the Program, understand its rationale and methodology, and be confronted with a decision on whether or not to participate. The following, then, is the substance of what was introduced to the students in the fall of 1985, and has been presented to other students subsequently.

> *Spiritual Friends is a program that offers to seminary students the opportunity of creating a covenant with a person in the Anderson area, with the aim being to make God more real particularly in the life of the student, but, ideally in the lives of both.*

> *The Program invites students to become accountable to another person, as together they seek to incorporate the spiritual disciplines into their lifestyle.*

> *Upon entering seminary, students are made aware of this Program, and are invited to participate. At no point is it offered as mandatory. But it is encouraged as crucial. The program is introduced during orientation sessions and students are invited by the Director of Spiritual Life to seek him out for further details, and the name of a potential Spiritual Friend. Students in the required course, "The Minister and Ministry," are again confronted with an opportunity to participate in the Program.*

> *From a list of Spiritual Friends, the student is given a name, address, and telephone number, along with other information as needed. The student then makes an appointment for an initial conference, at which a covenant*

is agreed upon that meets mutual needs and preferences. The student then reports to the Director that a relationship has begun.

These Friends are drawn from a wide spectrum of the Anderson Community. They include retired persons, pastors, agency executives, secretaries, housewives, teachers, senior seminary students, and others. They do not claim to be "great saints" nor experienced spiritual directors. They simply want to engage with another person in an attempt to make the life in Christ more real for both of them. And they have received a modest amount of orientation to the process involved in being a Spiritual Friend.

It is assumed that the student takes the initiative in establishing and maintaining this relationship. Before contacting a potential Friend, the student will have become familiar with the process of spiritual direction, read certain suggested material, and clarified personal spiritual goals and expectations of the relationship. At the first session, the student and Spiritual Friend will discuss and reach agreements around these and other concerns:

1. *Length, frequency, and place of meetings.*
2. *Mutual understandings and expectations of the process.*
3. *Agenda for future sessions (subject to change).*
4. *Accountability.*

Obviously, then, the first session will involve getting acquainted, reaching common grounds of understandings and expectation, setting goals, and asking for help. The student is the initiator and the friend is the facilitator. The task is to begin building a relationship that will later bear the weight of boredom (the continuing, repetitive aspects of spirituality), confrontation (being called to account, spiritually), and stress (pressures and obligations). So, it will take both persons working diligently to build the kind of relationship that will contribute to the spiritual growth of each participant.

The student will need to keep an accurate written summary of the covenant. In addition, she/he will find it advantageous to keep a journal-type record of goals that are set, disciplines practiced (prayer, meditation, confession, solitude, etc.) and personal responses (feelings, evidences of growth, insights, etc.) to private contemplative times, as well as sessions with the Spiritual Friend.

The Friend will seek to keep the focus of their sessions upon the student and his/her spiritual life. The main purpose is not for the student to air gripes, ventilate frustrations, nor seek to get counseling for personal problems. The Spiritual Friend is not a therapist, but may refer the student to another person for personal, relational, or psychological problems. An intervention frequently used by the Friend will be, "How is this affecting your prayer and devotional life?" Or, "Have you prayed about it?" Thus, the focus is not upon problem solving, insight, nor behavioral change, but upon spiritual resources and relationships.

It is essential that the student and Spiritual Friend work together to meet all appointments, keep faithful to beginning and ending times, eliminate distractions, prepare for each session appropriately, and find ways to affirm and express appreciation for each other. Each needs to be honest with the other and emotionally vulnerable. The student is not looking for a "model," but a "mentor." The Spiritual Friend is not looking for "perfection," but for a "pilgrim." Each session will likely include a few minutes of prayer for and with each other. But the main objective of each session is for the Friend to inquire of the student's spiritual disciplines and growth, and for the student to make herself/himself accountable to the Friend for her/his life in Christ.

An underlying assumption is that praying and growing spiritually works better when one receives good direction. To enter into an intentional relationship with a spiritual director, to the end that one may find that abundant life in Christ, may well be the wisest step one ever takes. To know God and be known by Him is a most basic human desire. The Spiritual Friends Program is a human contrivance devised to facilitate a process in which the Divine becomes a partner. You are to be commended for considering it. When would be a good time to begin?

This program was designed with Seminary students in mind, and this description took us into an institutional environment. However, it is hoped that this description will provide a model, and suggest a number of methods, that, with some revisions, might be adapted for use in other settings.

On Becoming A Spiritual Friend

A question that I pray will be asked by many who read this is: How can I become a spiritual friend to another person? For anyone who has experienced the gentle nudging of the Holy Spirit, extending an invitation to become a people helper, the question sounds familiar and almost inevitable. Many Christian social workers, psychotherapists, teachers, clergy, and others who invest their lives in the lives of others ask plaintively, "Isn't there more?" After having assisted in the feeding, housing, learning, and emotional adjustment of many persons, Christians in the helping professions often still feel a sense of emptiness. For deep down, they know that life consists of more than things, and knowledge, and mental health. It is then that they long to be able to help persons at a deeper level.

To become a spiritual friend does not require special training, though it might help. There is no single vocational track that leads one to this ministry, though there are several that make it more likely. There is not one personality type that qualifies a person, but certain types might find this work more natural. Let me gather a few random thoughts about how I see the idea of spiritual friends at work in the body of Christ.

First, I think that persons can better become spiritual friends one to another when their relationships are unencumbered by denominational hierarchy, ecclesiastical requirements, or institutional expectations. Spiritual direction is a charismatic practice, operating most purely when individuals are moved by the Spirit to seek a friend or to become a friend. To make spiritual direction a requirement for ordination, or graduation, or for continued employment, for example, is to do violence to the process, and perhaps, to the persons involved. But when two sincere believers on pilgrimage move toward one another with the hope that both of them will grow in the Lord, then some positive things can happen.

Second, I think that persons can better become spiritual friends one to another when their relationship is as nearly egalitarian as possible. The notion of being ''under direction'' is just not a very acceptable one from contemporary theological, psychological, and cultural perspectives. A spiritual relationship works better, I suggest, when each party has feelings of equality and collegiality. Of course, these are elusive concepts! In actual practice, one person is likely to be a little older, more experienced vocationally, or more advanced spiritually. After all, common sense dictates that we seek out that sort of person! It is unrealistic to expect absolute equality, but if the differences can become less of an issue, the chances are increased that the relationship will become more mutually caring, supportive, and intimate. While this relationship need not be based on ''chumminess'' and social compatibility, there must be profound respect and care for each other, and a deep level of trust.

Third, I think persons can better become spiritual friends one to another, when the director has matured or advanced spiritually to the place that he/she can provide qualified guidance for the directee. Is that a contradiction to what I just said above? Not necessarily. Ideally, what I think works best is this: In an egalitarian spiritual relationship, the "equality" is primarily a matter of attitude and social dynamics, but it is fairly obvious which is the director and which the directee. On some occasions, when factors of age, experience, and maturity do not make the roles obvious, then the two persons may, by mutual consent, decide who is the helper and who is the helpee. To further complicate the description of an egalitarian relationship, note that the two persons may, by mutual consent, reverse roles. Then the directee, becomes the director. It seems to me that an egalitarian relationship as described here has the ingredients for long-term benefits. In the final analysis, though, my hunch is that most spiritual friendships will proceed in the more traditional manner, where one person is clearly the director and the other the directee, and they both stay in those roles.

Fourth, I think persons can better become spiritual friends one to another, when the director has reached the age when spiritual, emotional, and physical maturity are most likely to have occurred. What age do I mean? That is a tough question, but my guess is, over 40. There is nothing magic about that age, of course, but prior to it, it seems that most young adults are preoccupied with exterior concerns — job, family, success. Only after some or most of these issues are resolved, or nearly so, do persons turn to interior concerns. Of course, there are many notable exceptions. But, as a general rule, I think that persons past mid-life are more likely to make more effective spiritual directors.

Fifth, and finally, I think that persons can better become spiritual friends one to another when the theological assumptions of both incline more toward grace than law. Of course, an adequate and balanced theology of both grace and law are essential for spiritual growth. But my observation is that people who have a rigid, legalistic approach to Christian living carry within themselves a lot of guilt, and frequently hide their deepest selves from others. They frequently set extremely high standards of holy living for themselves and for those around them. Their penchant for pure doctrine often keeps them in a sort of bondage, based on more good works and more perfect performance.

Now, I'm not lobbying for a careless or compromising response to doctrine. I am, however, suggesting that grace is a perfectly good doctrine which is often neglected, and the practice of it is necessary if one is to grow spiritually. The beginning point of growth is the admission of the need for it. Until we acknowledge honestly our failures, fears, and needs, and confess them openly to God (and maybe to a spiritual director also), very little cleansing and growth is likely to take place. To pretend health is to remain sick. Those of us in the holiness tradition, especially, need to be reminded that confession is good for the soul, even after conversion.

Sometimes, admission of weakness is a benefit. When we acknowledge our weaknesses, we are more likely to seek a physician — whether of the soul, body, or mind. As long as we pretend that we are not sick (or sinful, or needy), we won't turn for help, choosing rather the hypocritical posture of "I'm OK," or "I can handle this by myself."

When we can acknowledge our spiritual poverty, own it as ours without blaming anybody else, realize that we cannot lift ourselves by our bootstraps, then we are ready to turn to a spiritual friend for guidance and support.

There really is a lot of difference between Christian perfection and psychological perfectionism — though we tend to muddy them together. Perfection (theologically) has to do with wholeness and completeness which is accomplished by our relationship with Jesus Christ. It is not something we work up or achieve by human effort. It is a free gift of grace. On the other hand, psychological perfectionism has to do with incompleteness, inadequacy, and drivenness to accomplish the impossible. It is a human corruption of the concept of holiness. Christians, trying too hard to become perfect (in the wrong way), often fall victim to perfectionism.

Grace helps us sort all that out. It reminds us of God's love for us even when we are imperfect. Grace reminds us that we don't have to do anything in order to glorify God and please God. We cannot earn our salvation. But we were created in the image of God who is pleased by who we are. Our call is to be true to who we are — human, subject to faults, but created for wholeness.

Characteristics Of An Effective Spiritual Friend

The question, "How can I become a spiritual friend to another person?" is still before us. I am not really sure that it is appropriate for one to set out to become a spiritual director. There seems to be a bit of incongruity to suggest that one may "hang out a shingle." Instead, it seems that one appropriately becomes a spiritual friend by being sought out. *If* you are being sought out for guidance; *if* you experience a sense of fulfillment as you do the work; *if* persons are genuinely being helped; and *if* your director discerns with you that what you are doing is proper — then you are a spiritual director. That sounds almost too simplistic. But I think it works that way.

There are some insights, skills, and personal characteristics (together, they make up one's potential for this ministry) which can be developed and sharpened in order for the director to grow increasingly more effective. Let me identify these potentialities in a sort of checklist fashion. Answer these questions honestly, and they may help you discern whether or not you are the kind of person who could be useful to God in this work. You may want to work through these questions with your journal at hand, or with your spiritual friend, or both.

1. Are you aware of a call to and gifts for the work of spiritual direction?

2. Have you made a deep commitment to a disciplined, lifelong inward journey?

3. Are you dedicated to the cultivation of your mystical faculties, and are you willing to follow appropriate ascetical practices?

4. Are you willing to apply yourself to continuing your

education, particularly in the areas of spiritual theology, the behavioral sciences, biblical studies, and counseling?

5. Do you currently have a qualified spiritual friend with whom you are discussing these matters?

6. Do you lead a disciplined life of prayer, including meditation and deep relaxation?

7. Do you regularly read the Scriptures and devotional classics in a reflective, contemplative manner, including a disciplined regimen of inductive Bible study?

8. Do you keep a journal in order to record your perceptions of God's movement in your life and to note your communications with Him?

9. Are you a part of a small group dedicated to prayer, study, sharing, and mutual accountability?

10. Is corporate worship a priority for you?

11. Do you periodically devote yourself to fasting, retreats, expressions of love, solitude, and other disciplines that you personally have found to be rewarding?

12. Do you have ways to regularly witness to your faith and seek to lead others to the joy that you have found in Christ?

13. Are you involved in service to persons in your community and in the wider world?

14. Are you conscientiously involved in, or working on, at least some of the twenty-six disciplines listed in Chapter II?

Do you feel inclined toward a ministry of spiritual direction? Do you know of people who need a spiritual friend, and you seem to be the logical choice? But you feel a little intimidated by my list of questions, don't you? Now would be a good time to claim grace! Don't get under a burden of guilt just because you still have some learning and growing to do. Keep in mind that God "knows our frame, and remembers that we are dust" (Psalms 103:14).

Over the years, I've seen many lists (and composed a few!) of the qualities of an effective minister, and I've been intimidated by most of them. I've often felt that I was not "qualified" for the ministry. Either I didn't know enough, or I lacked some skill, or my personality wasn't quite the type needed for the situation. I've made my share of excuses.

But we don't have to be good enough, or capable enough. We never are, anyway! The best and most effective ministers are available persons, through whom God can work. If you can stay out of the way, and stay usable, God will make you useful. So, even if you didn't score A + on all fourteen of the questions above, just commit who you *are*, and what you *can* do, to God's will. I believe God can use you!

Informal Direction

One other important thing needs to be said about being a spiritual friend. Much of the spiritual direction which we do, takes place when we're hardly even aware that we're doing it. Our response to questions, offhanded comments, spontaneous prayers with people, conversations on the street, words of encouragement over a cup of coffee, a warm handshake after the service — these and other informal contacts may serve as spiritual direction. This is unplanned, unstructured direction, but it is valid and important.

This is ministry on-the-go, but often it is exactly what is needed. The essential features of this kind of informal direction are two in number: (1) Did the minister intentionally inquire about the spiritual state of the person? (2) Did the person experience the minister as being aware of and concerned for his/her spiritual state? It doesn't always take an hour for this to happen.

The difficult part for the minister (director) is to be sensitive to persons, so tuned in to them as to be able to listen to the messages behind the words, or behind the masks. Sometimes a question in the hallway, or an inquiring phone call, is all that is needed to convey concern, and, perhaps, lead to a deeper discussion. The simple question, "How is it with you and God?" when asked and answered from the depths, serve to remind the two persons what the Christian life really is all about. And that question, pointed though it is, should be as natural for a caring Christian as it is for a physician to ask a patient, "How do you feel today?"

Finding A Spiritual Friend

Now that we have examined the essentials of being a spiritual friend to someone else, let us think about finding a friend for ourselves. I frequently hear people say, "I just don't know anybody I could trust that much," or "There's not anyone experienced in this work, that I know of, in my community." Those statements may be true for a few people. But they may be excuses used by those who are reluctant to trust another human being, or who haven't seriously looked for a director. And they may contain a little bit of resistance to the whole idea of spiritual direction!

The fact is, there are quite a few people available to function as spiritual guides. If our approach to finding a spiritual friend is more like one beggar asking another beggar where to find bread, then our search is likely to be fruitful. If you are seriously seeking a spiritual director, here are some things to keep in mind:

1. If it really is God's will for you to have a spiritual friend, God will make her/him available to you. So, pray about it and wait for God's leading.

2. Don't avoid direction just because it doesn't "feel good" to you. This may be internal resistance to something new and threatening. Furthermore, you need to use reason and good judgment in making a decision as well as praying about it and relying on your intuition.

3. What are your reasons for seeking spiritual direction *now*? Is it to make you a better minister? To please ecclesiastical superiors? To cure burnout? The appropriate reasons to engage in intentional spiritual formation are (a) To worship God more wholly; (b) To know God more completely; and (c) To serve people more effectively. To seek spiritual direction

because it is trendy, is not an adequate justification. To seek it as an economical way of getting psychotherapy, is inappropriate, if not unethical.

4. In launching your search, look first among the clergy and members of religious orders. This is not to say that persons in religious vocations are the best qualified, or that they are the most effective. This is just to identify a likely source. Many Protestant pastors, especially those who are seminary educated, may be able to serve in this capacity, or they could refer you to someone else. In many cases you may find it necessary to cross over denominational lines. There are some distinct advantages to this. To move into an unfamiliar environment adds a dimension of intentionality and formality to the arrangement.

5. Your request for spiritual direction might be denied. Try not to feel rejected. People *are* busy, and not everyone who seems to be capable of this ministry is ready for it now. So, keep asking. In a few situations, you may need to offer a modest honorarium, or, at least, some kind of gift.

6. In many congregations there are dedicated lay persons who have received spiritual direction and would be ready to guide someone else. In a telephone call to the pastor, you might secure the information you need.

7. Whenever necessary, or whenever it is appropriate, try a more casual approach to spiritual direction. I am aware that in my descriptions and discussions I have made spiritual direction sound quite formal, structured, professional, and complicated. And I did that quite intentionally in order to set forth what I consider to be the optimum practice of the discipline. I have wanted to show you the best, knowing that frequently we have to settle for what is available. Much of our lives are spent ''making do,'' or ''living in the meantime.''

So, if you can't locate that first-rate, trained, experienced director, do the best you can. Make a covenant with another Christian on pilgrimage, to mutually encourage, support, and guide each other along the way. It need not be all that complicated. Just agree to share your spiritual lives, and what you together know about growth. Become spiritual friends!

8. Understand the process. Do some reading, reflecting, and praying, before you contact a potential director. Then, up-front, say, "This is new to me. How do we begin?" You can learn about the process as you begin to pray.

9. Expect to learn, stretch, grow, hurt, fail, and try again. The relationship may not always be easy, comfortable, and friendly. As to your own spiritual state, you'll likely go through some dry times. Keep an open mind and a willing spirit.

10. Refine and revise your expectations as you go along. Goals may need to be changed. Discuss these revisions fully with your director.

Conclusion

As we come to the end of this discussion on spiritual direction, let me review what I think is the proper approach for those who may be considering the possibility of entering into it. This is not a decision that should be made casually. It should not be made unilaterally. The presentation of oneself for spiritual direction should be the culmination of a process that, (a) began with the prompting of the Spirit; (b) included conversations with family, friends, pastors, significant others; and (c) gave evidence of studied sensitivity towards one's denominational and congregational beliefs and traditions.

There is a sense in which the decision to enter into a spiritual friendship on an intentional basis, *is* a very private matter. But it is also a communal concern. As Christians, we are part of a Body, and responsible to it. As ministers, we have experienced a common calling. As pastors, we belong to a professional fraternity. We really do need to link hearts and hands with those around us when we undertake this sort of venture. There really is no place for secrecy, or independence, or arbitrary decisions in the ministry — and that includes our participation in spiritual direction.

Spiritual direction is not just for the bad times. It is for all times. Unless we learn to rely on others, however, to form a team (support network) to undergird our ministry, to seek nurturance on a continuing basis, we become candidates for major depression, physical illness, or moral failure. I deeply believe that spiritual direction is one method that we and the Holy Spirit can use together, to defeat the enemy of our souls, whose work it is to confuse sincere believers and destroy the churches.

In this chapter, I have tried to define spiritual direction, offer some glimpses of some of the ways it has been practiced, and provide a justification for it from a variety of perspectives. The Spiritual Friends Program at the Anderson School of Theology was described in order to provide one model for the practice of spiritual direction. Some suggestions for finding a spiritual director, and becoming a directee, concluded the chapter.

Now what? What do you plan to do about spiritual direction? My hope is that you have responded positively to the idea of spiritual direction as one of the essential disciplines in your own spiritual formation. Beyond that, I pray that you may soon experience the fulfillment of a nurturing support system, which includes a very special spiritual friend.

IV

Accountability

*Therefore confess your sins to one another and pray
for one another, that you may be healed (James 5:16).*

In the free church tradition, we have valued our individuality, but, sadly, have often neglected our call to mutual responsibility. In this chapter we will examine the importance of being accountable. To become accountable is to accept the responsibility of being answerable.

As Christians we are called to give an account of ourselves before God. In practice, however, this ideal easily degenerates into an individualistic following of one's own conscience without benefit of the corrective of Scripture and spiritual community. My concern for accountability includes the whole family of God. But primarily, this chapter addresses the need for accountability among Christian leaders, and pastors particularly.

Experience has shown that some form of disciplined preparation is needed before persons are placed in leadership positions. In some cases the church has been careless at this point — too quick to put willing but ill-prepared persons into places of responsibility for which they were not spiritually, mentally, and emotionally ready. Most professions require extensive preparation in required areas of study. To make the study of history, for example, optional in a college curriculum, is to insure the presence of persons inadequately educated in history, come graduation day. Some students (perhaps many) would, in concession to the flesh, opt out of all history classes! So, requirements are printed in the catalogue. If it is as important to be spiritually formed as it is to be informed about history, perhaps it *is* time the churches found ways to require specific preparation for those who would serve in ministry, and especially those seeking ordination. This preparation needs to go beyond subjects and skills and focus on character development.

One of the surprising discoveries that many pastors report is just how much freedom they do have in their work. They don't need to punch a clock. They decide when their days off will be, and they schedule their own appointments. They generally have a lot of flexibility in designing their ministry (programs, goals, resources, calendar, and so on) in a given context. (I am thinking primarily of free church pastors, though what I am saying is generally true for ministers throughout Christendom, I think.) So, it is not unusual, especially for beginning ministers, to think and ask, "What shall I do?" "When shall I begin?" "How shall I do it?" (A wiser and more mature pastor might change the "I's" to "We's"!)

Let's agree, then, that there really is plenty of opportunity for the spirit of individualism, or the Lone Ranger approach to ministry, but this attitude is dangerous. In my opinion, a great number of leaders yearn to function in a collegial manner, perfectly willing, even desiring, to become appropriately accountable. Can anything be said for those who are *not* motivated by ego, and who deeply desire to belong to a fraternity of servants, accountable to God, their church, and to each other? The answer is yes! There is a great interest in accountability, and there are some good models available. Let's explore the possibilities together.

By definition, accountability means to be answerable to, or responsible to; to give an explanation for one's behavior; to report; to evaluate; to be under contract. The opposite of accountability is irresponsibility. From the ministerial perspective, we may think of two kinds of accountability: *Imposed*, meaning the requirements or expectations handed down by others; or *Voluntary*, meaning a self-initiated, intentional sort of accountability. In this chapter, my primary concern is to address the issue of voluntary accountability in spirituality. It needs to be noted, however, that it is difficult to define the parameters of spiritual accountability with precision, inasmuch as spirituality touches on the whole of life.

What follows, then, is a series of suggestions for the person who is seeking to grow in this matter of voluntary spiritual accountability. It is not likely that the professional ministry will ever be as strictly managed (educational requirements, code of ethics, professional identification, and so on) as, for example, is the case with medical doctors. But many persons feel that the profession is in need of more careful management in order to insure integrity. My hope is that we will discover more intrinsic motivations to "professionalize" the profession (and we'll probably do that on a one by one basis), rather than waiting for extrinsic factors (judicatories, a great public outcry, or whatever) to force us to upgrade our profession.

I. If you wish to grow in voluntary spiritual accountability, develop a practical theology of accountability that can be applied to your life and ministry.

I think it was Ralph Sockman who claimed that his primary task as a pastor was to comfort the afflicted and afflict the comfortable. My observation is that ministers, generally, are more inclined toward comforting than toward afflicting. As evidence I point to the abundance of literature in the area of pastoral care, but to the paucity of literature in the area of righteous discipline.

Pastors, by and large, are well-read, well-equipped, and highly motivated with regard to pastoral care. But when it comes to pastoral discipline and prophetic preaching, we suddenly get a severe case of shyness. We try to call it humility, but it is probably reluctance!

And if we're "easy" on the people, how much more likely are we to be "easy" on ourselves? Ministers really do need to be nurtured and supported on occasion, but there are also times when we need to be corrected and chastened. Traditionally, we haven't policed our ranks very carefully, so we have had our Elmer Gantry-types periodically, as well as others whose indiscretions were less notorious. The vast majority of the members of the clergy are, of course, decent, hard working, faithful types. It is the infrequent exception who gets a lot of ink and air time, thus, causing the public to feel that the most recent disclosure is typical.

In quest of a theology of accountability, one might first turn to the book of Jude. Apparently, it was written to defend the faith against some influential persons who were guilty of corrupt doctrine and practice. While the epistle contains strong denunciations, it also breathes with a tender love and a strong hope. It is thought that the evil teaching (v. 4) had to do with antinomianism, the idea that Christians were free from observing the law. There must have been a few people in the infant church who had problems accepting authority! That has a contemporary ring, doesn't it? And a strikingly appropriate message, dealing with persons who cause divisions (v. 19) in the church, is delivered by the writer. (Now might be a good time to read the Book of Jude, reflect on it, and do some writing in your journal.)

Also, I would suggest a careful study of 1 and 2 Timothy and Titus, being particularly alert to the themes of admonition, exhortation, reproof, rebuke, correction, and instruction. A superficial study of these scriptures may lead one to conclude that Paul was giving directions to pastors about their ministry of admonition with the laity. No doubt that is a major part of the writer's concern. But a more careful analysis will reveal that this ministry of calling one another to accountability was to be exercised throughout the church — laity to laity, pastor to laity, laity to pastor, and pastor to pastor. References to pastoral admonition may also be found in Romans, Colossians, and 1 Thessalonians.

Thomas Oden, in his excellent textbook on *Pastoral The-ology: Essentials of Ministry*, provides a helpful chapter on pastoral admonition. He describes the work of pastoral cor-rection and discipline as something the pastor does to the peo-ple, under the direction of the Holy Spirit. The chapter is fourteen pages long. But his comments on pastoral accounta-bility is limited to one page. I am not trying to take anything away from a well written book, one that has been very help-ful to me. My fear is, this seems to be rather typical. There seems to be more interest in teaching pastors to be responsi-ble for the souls of their congregation than to be responsible for their own soul. The pastor calls others to accountability, but who calls her/him to accountability?

Pastor, to whom are you, as of this moment, *really* account-able? To God, you say? Fine. But aren't you glad your physi-cian is responsible to the American Medical Association for his/her level of expertise and overall performance? Aren't you glad teachers have to prove their ability to teach and fitness for the classroom by obtaining a degree and professional cer-tification? After ordination, who examines you, pastor? Who evaluates your ministerial performance? Who inquires of your work-style, and life-style, and prayer-style? Is there a place for peer admonition? Are there ever any occasions when a con-gregation ought to admonish a pastor? Wouldn't it be better voluntarily to design a method by which one can seek to be-come accountable in ministry?

II. If you wish to grow in voluntary spiritual accountability, develop an orientation to ministry that is conducive to the no-tion of collegiality.

Accountability works better when it is sought, rather than imposed. So, my suggestion is, be open to becoming part of a team. Recite as a litany, until it becomes part of the fabric of your personality: "We're in this together; we really do need each other; together we can do what none of us can do alone; I am totally engaged with my peers and with my faith group." Keep on repeating the litany. Think, read, and pray about the basic message of it. You may need to work with a mentor, or spiritual friend, or supervisor, or psychotherapist, about your fear or your resistance to collegiality. Become convinced in your mind and heart that, to be a part of a team accountable to a coach and sponsor, is a truer metaphor of Christian ministry than is the solitary warrior doing lonely battle against the forces of evil.

I'm not sure I know how to develop this relational/collegial orientation to ministry except to understand that it really is the way that Jesus had in mind for us. He called the twelve "to be with Him" (Mark 3:14). He sent out the disciples (Mark 6:12) and the seventy (Luke 10:1) in teams of two, and they returned to Jesus to share what had happened to them (Mark 6:30).

Once we become committed to Jesus' archetypal model for collegial ministry, then we can begin working to change intellectual assumptions, structures, and traditions, in order to make our ministries more effective. For some of us, such a basic change in our theology of ministry may come very slowly, and with great difficulty. Such a radical reorientation in perspective may require the assistance of a mentor or a spiritual friend. To exchange an individualistic approach to ministry for a cooperative approach is no small undertaking. But I believe that it will be worth it!

Let me at this point say, somewhat parenthetically, that I recommend personal, in-depth psychotherapy for all ministers who are committed to growth, and who anticipate doing counseling as part of their ministry. In learning to *be* a counselor, it is essential to *get* counseling. Isn't it interesting that we pastors often recommend or even seek to give medicine to our parishioners that we aren't willing to take for ourselves?

I suppose we're talking about vulnerability — making ourselves available to others, open to their evaluation, or guidance, or assistance. It helps to admit that we aren't self-sufficient. It also helps to reach out. Even leaders need a warm, strong hand from someone who will guide and sustain us.

III. If you wish to grow in voluntary spiritual accountability, develop a support network for ministry.

I often hear ministers and spouses speak of their loneliness. Many have shared with me their feelings that no one really understands their situation, and that they don't know anyone well enough to trust them with their feelings. One of the myths of ministry (perpetuated by pastors and laity alike) is that ministers are supposed to be strong, enthusiastic, successful, and pure — which means that they *never* experience weakness, discouragement, failure, nor sin. The impossible dream!

Because we are human, there needs to be some systematic way for every minister to deal with human frailty. Of course we always have available to us the rich spiritual resources of grace, prayer, and the Word of God. I would not knowingly minimize the value of this vertical dimension to our health and effectiveness. But speaking humanly, I know the value, too, of the horizontal dimension. I was a pastor for about eighteen years, and I remember the feelings of loneliness, needing to turn somewhere for help, but not knowing where to turn. Not only did I not know *where* (or to whom) to turn, but it seemed inappropriate for me to *have* to turn for help. After all, I was ordained, and I *couldn't* let anyone know I was experiencing difficulties! Have you ever had any feelings like that? Roy Oswald says one pastor described his job this way: "I feel like a chunk of cheese from which everyone wants just a nibble." See Roy M. Oswald, *Clergy Self-Care: Finding a Balance for Effective Ministry* (Alban Institute, 1991). Oswald describes a number of self-care strategies, including spiritual depth, support systems, psychotherapy, assertiveness, laughter, and detachment. His many years of ministry enable him to write helpfully.

Support Network

If you have had such feelings, or in anticipation of such

experiences yet to come, let's talk about a support network. *For a rationale, one simple sentence will suffice: I need others in order to make it in the ministry.* Believe me, that is a true statement! While it is true that ministers need people, ministers can become emotionally and spiritually sick because of people. We need to tend our connections with a few people in order to help us survive the masses of people. So, make it easy on yourself. Admit your needs. Reach out. Accept support.

Are you ready to build, revise, or strengthen your support network? I suggest that you take a sheet of paper, or turn in your journal, and let's work on a support network.

A. First, think through your rationale. You need good reasons for doing whatever you do. Remember this axiom: Methodology roots in theology. Respond in writing to these questions:

1. Why do I need a support network?
2. What is my theological/biblical rationale for a support network?
3. Why have I decided to act *now*?

B. Second, list the names of persons who are, or who could be part of your network. (List several names for each category.)

1. Family Members (wife, husband, parents, children)
2. Close associates (staff members, lay leaders, peers)
3. Significant others (friends, teachers, pastors)
4. Available denominational leaders (judicatory officials, agency representatives, board members)
5. Available community resources (schools, churches, police, service agencies, library, helping professionals)
6. Available consultants (persons who can provide resources or guidance to you, as needed)

C. Third, write out your proposed method of contacting some or all the persons listed above, soliciting their help, and cultivating the relationship. You are creating a Covenant of Ministry with these persons. Make it clear to them what you are attempting to do, and how you believe they might be able to help you. Telephone calls, letters, and personal conversations will assist you in the process. Beware of leaning too heavily on family members.

D. Fourth, set some attainable goals.

1. How do I need to grow and develop as a minister? One of my projects this year will be *me.* What (who) do I want to become?

2. In what specific ways will I call upon the several members of my network?

3. How will I evaluate the effectiveness of my network, and revise it as needed?

4. What will be my intellectual (examples: theology, sociology, Bible, psychology, missions) growing edge this year?

5. What will be my practical ministries (examples: worship, evangelism, homiletics, leadership) growing edge his year?

E. Fifth, form a support group. It is assumed that your network includes a number of persons who are at some emotional or geographical distance from you. Thus, a more intimate group is needed, a small group immediately available to you. This might be three to five persons with whom you could get together regularly for prayer, fellowship, sharing, and mutual guidance. List their names.

F. Finally, find a mentor. This person may or may not be a member of your support group, but likely is listed as part of your network. This is the one person you turn to as spiritual guide, soul friend, or supervisor.

I suggest that you reflect on the idea of a Support Network. Pray about it and discuss it with someone you trust. You might want to do additional reading in this area, or gather more information. If so, see Appendix F. The United Methodist Church, through its General Board of Discipleship, provides information about Covenant Discipleship Groups. In addition, the Division of Ordained Ministry has prepared a Spiritual

Formation Resource packet. Both contain good ideas about support groups and accountability.

Models And Mentors

There is a lot being said these days about finding adequate role models in ministry, and I understand the need. I interpret a ministerial "model" to be a person who embodies nearly all of our idealizations about ministry in a nearly perfect balance. A model is someone we can admire and emulate. My problem with models is that they often are chosen on the basis of their glamour. From a distance, they appear successful and spiritual. Let this person preach a few impressive sermons, lead a scintillating conference, write a book, or report some glowing church statistics, and all the young pastors around rush to imitate. But to copy someone else's style and philosophy *could* prove disastrous.

What is needed, I think, is not a model, but a mentor. A mentor can get closer to you than the model. You can get involved at the growing level with a mentor. You have a mentor, if you have a significant other who:

> *cares about you as a person;*
> *guides you to growth resources;*
> *listens to you in a disciplined manner;*
> *prays with and for you;*
> *confronts you firmly, but lovingly;*
> *provides encouragement;*
> *cultivates your creativity;*
> *tutors your learnings;*
> *directs your development of spiritual disciplines;*
> *assists you in examining your motives;*
> *demonstrates hope and optimism.*

Wouldn't you like to have a relationship like this? Most ministers don't need role models nearly as much as they need a warm friend, some timely support, a bit of wise advice, a reassurance that they are professionally valued — in short, they need a mentor.

Is a mentor the same as a spiritual director? Possibly. It seems to me that a mentor, a spiritual director, a spiritual friend, and a soul friend could be the same person. I'm using the terms interchangeably. Basically, what is needed is that a mentor be:

1. **Safe.** That is, not one who might have to do ecclesiastical evaluations, nor one who violates confidentiality, nor one who tends to be punitive.

2. **Caring.** One who is accepting, affirming, gentle, loving by nature.

3. **Available.** One who can be scheduled and is an emotionally available (expressive, responsive, empathetic) person.

4. **Experienced.** One who has experience in people-helping.

5. **Hopeful.** One who is optimistic, believes in you!

In summary, a mentor is one with whom you can share your life and ministry. It really isn't so much the *unknown* that limits our ministry as it is the *unuttered*. When we close ourselves off from others who could help us, choosing to flounder in lonely frustration, we delay effective ministry, and may eventually destroy it.

Several years ago, during an intake session with a young woman who became a counselee of mine, she reported feeling totally helpless and hopeless. I suggested that she relax, not try so hard to make life work, and let me do the hoping for her for awhile. When I expressed my willingness to hope for her, she burst into tears, grabbed my hands, and thanked me profusely. I *did* hope for her, and eventually she regained her optimism and was able to go on with life. Is your support network in place? Don't wait until you are desperate. It is difficult to build a support network when the pressure is up.

IV. If you wish to grow in voluntary spiritual accountability, gather all the information about yourself that you possible can.

Leaders need to know who they are. How can we expect to know God at the deeper levels, and know other persons well enough to minister to them, if we do not first know ourselves? I'm not talking about sentimental, subjective, self-absorption. I'm talking about using all the resources, information, diagnostic procedures, and such like that are available to us in order to enhance our self-awareness. I'm inviting us to apply reason and common sense to the process of self-evaluation.

Feedback

One rather simple way to grow in self-awareness, especially at the point of knowing how others perceive us, or how we "come across," is to seek feedback. When others give us feedback, they hold up a mirror, as it were, allowing us to see ourselves as they see us. Feedback is generally more useful when we ask for it, than when it is forced upon us. We can use feedback to determine the accuracy of our communication, whether or not our behavior is interpreted by others in the manner we intended, and what impact our voice, appearance, mannerisms, or leadership style have upon persons. (Refer to Appendix A.)

In order to invite feedback, one might take a sheet of paper, write several questions on it (see next page), hand it to a trusted friend, mentor, or church leader, and encourage the person to provide totally honest responses. A sit-down conversation would enable you and the feedback giver to discuss the comments and perceptions as written, plus some discussion on ways you might change and grow. Actually, the feedback giver need not be one who knows you well. In that case the feedback becomes more in the order of first impressions, or surface reactions. But persons who spend their lives initiating a lot of contacts, and are frequently "up front," really do need to know how they are initially perceived by others. Sometimes we do not get second chances to redeem ourselves!

The sheet of questions with space for responses handed to an acquaintance or church member might include some or all of the following:

1. How do you see me as a person? How do I come across? Describe typical mannerisms.

2. What do you experience when you are around me? How do you generally feel in my presence?

3. How do I come across as a pastor/teacher? What seems to be the feeling tone of the people while I'm up front?

4. Please give me suggestions for growth and improvement:
   a. How can I come across as a warmer, friendlier person?
   b. What might help my preaching delivery?
   c. What about my personal appearance?
   d. What about my professional demeanor?

Are you ready for that kind of honest confrontation? You could probably handle it and process it better with a mentor or a colleague group. And, you need to remember that not everyone is capable of giving you that kind of feedback. Their ego-strength might not permit it, or their understanding of the relationship between clergy and laity might forbid it. Good friends may be reluctant to risk the friendship. The results always need to be interpreted, but the first order of business is to accept the feedback as valid from their perspective, understand it as fully as you can, then consider ways to use it.

Persons giving feedback might remember that:

1. Feedback needs to be more descriptive than evaluative. Observe, describe, and share, but don't judge.

2. Specific vocabulary is better than general. To say "you are a dominant personality" is not as effective as saying, "in the meeting last night when you said ... I felt pressure to agree with you."

3. It is better to give feedback about behavior or attitudes which can be modified. It doesn't help to be reminded of a shortcoming or a situation over which one has no control.

4. Good timing helps. Sometimes feedback may need to

be delayed. Or, perhaps the feedback needs to follow some words of affirmation or support.

5. The feedback was requested with sincerity, and a desire to grow. Let it be returned that way. Gentleness and strength always make good partners.

6. It is important to provide time for clarification and discussion of the feedback, when the receiver asks for it.

Ministers who are open to critique, who invite feedback from others, are more likely to become voluntarily accountable than are those who are suspicious of evaluation and prefer not to present themselves for candid review. Are you sufficiently self-aware to know which you prefer? Are you open to making some changes?

Tests And Surveys

Many seminaries, judicatories, and ordination committees require a comprehensive testing program prior to admission, placement, or recommendation for ordination, respectively. Even if you are not subject to such a requirement, avail yourself of the opportunity. A thorough testing program, accompanied with qualified and sensitive interpretation, will enable you to discover your strengths, weaknesses, tendencies, needs, preferences, and such like. You really do need such information before you embark on your professional ministry. You will gain a lot of information about yourself, and better be able to understand why people respond to you as they do.

As a minimum package, I would suggest that you find a way to take the Minnesota Multiphasic Personality Inventory (MMPI), the Myers-Briggs Type Inventory (MBTI), and the FIRO-B. A qualified Christian psychologist can assist you in taking these and getting appropriate interpretations.

The "Profiles in Ministry" program, prepared under the direction of the Association of Theological Schools, is available at most seminaries. This will give the person a great deal of insight into the ways she/he functions in a variety of ministerial settings and situations.

There are many other less sophisticated evaluative surveys and questionnaires that could be used, preferably with the guidance of a mentor or support group. As examples, let me refer you to Appendix G for a "Pastoral Self-Analysis," and to Appendix H, for a "Minister's Self-Rating Scale." These are rather uncomplicated instruments which I prepared for use in seminary classes. You might want to check on the "Pastoral Evaluation Guide" in Moreman, *Developing Spiritually and Professionally* (Westminster, 1984) p. 107, and "The Clergy Questionnaire," in Warlick, *How to be a Minister and a Human Being* (Judson Press, 1982) p. 117. I have added as Appendix F, a list of resources for ministers, which includes information about various types of test materials.

Myers-Briggs Type Inventory

This is not the place to attempt a detailed discussion of the MBTI as it relates to self-understanding. Such a discussion would require a description of the information which one gains by taking it, plus an introduction to Carl Jung's theory on personality types, on which the MBTI is based. I do hope to motivate you to look further at this helpful instrument.

I have used it for several years with seminary classes, and find it to be an excellent tool for identifying how one prefers to function in ministry. Of course, the raw data has to be translated into ministry paradigms, and applied to the person's own situation. It is a positive instrument, for it encourages the taker to value his/her characteristics or differences. It has powerful implications for preaching, worship leading, working with groups, and private prayer. I have also used it with couples and families as they seek better to understand how they function in relationship to each other. It is currently popular for pastor's conferences to offer the MBTI and an interpretation that relates it to ministry. Watch for such an opportunity. I highly recommend it!

For further study of psychological types, I recommend particularly these three books:

Kiersey and Bates, *Please Understand Me.*

Michael and Norrisey, *Prayer and Temperament.*

Faucett and Faucett, *Personality and Spiritual Freedom.*

The Center for Application of Psychological Type (see Appendix F for an address) has some very helpful material on types and spirituality.

How might personality typology be useful to ministers and the church? It helps us know ourselves better, recognize ways that we are different from others, and cherish those differences. When we know our strengths or preferences, we can work more efficiently by capitalizing on them. When we understand that some forms of prayer more naturally fit our personality type, then we can quit feeling guilty that we don't find all the other forms of prayer equally rewarding.

Leaders will be more effective when they have some basic understanding of their own preferences, behaviors, and emotional responses. Furthermore, to be able to identify and value the uniqueness of others will help us avoid the tendency to squeeze others into our molds. The MBTI helps us see how very different we are, but how these differences can be complementary in the Body of Christ.

Spiritual Gifts

One of the significant areas of self-understanding, in my opinion, is an awareness of one's spiritual giftedness coupled with an understanding of how to use gifts effectively in the church. Once one has gained an adequate grasp of the theology of the Holy Spirit's gifts, one is ready to use an inventory or a questionnaire to help identify one's particular gifts. Appendix E contains a study guide, a list of some practical theological questions relating to the gifts, and some suggestions for further reading. Appendix F contains the address of the Fuller Institute of Evangelism and Church Growth, from whom several spiritual gifts questionnaires are available.

When a pastor knows her/his gift-mix, ministry can then be based more on giftedness than on stereotype, or on the expectations of others. For me it was liberating when I was able to assume accountability for the wise use of my gifts, and at the same time reject the guilt I often felt for not doing everything that other ministers were doing.

The church was intended by God to be a volunteer organism. And it functions in a more healthy, growing fashion when the base of volunteers is broadened. In fact, *all* believers should find a place of involvement in a local congregation. Saints were not called to be spectators! But, who coordinates this involvement? And, what about motivation?

In seeking to answer those two troublesome questions, let me first suggest a clue to understanding motivation. I think it is a potentially dangerous notion. Motivation smacks of *man*ipulation and *man*dates and *man*agement. Too often it means the many under control of a few. The problem is, there is often too much *man* in motivation! Why not let the Holy Spirit motivate persons? Most other forms of motivation may be unworthy of the church.

As to coordination, it is my firm conviction that there is no more efficient and effective approach to church administration than this: Let there be a pastor who has the gifts of leadership-administration-faith (at least one), who is devoted to helping believers identify and enhance their particular gifts, and who is willing to engage with the congregation in the deployment of all gifts. In most settings this will be a growing congregation — by whatever standard one measures growth.

V. If you wish to grow in voluntary spiritual accountability, redefine your ecclesiastical connections.

I will say more about the church and spiritual formation in Chapter 6, but in passing, let me raise a few of the issues that confront us as we struggle to face the conflicts that inevitably arise between our membership in the Kingdom and our loyalty to a denomination or faith group.

Kingdom theology often has an esoteric air to it — idealistic, intellectual, historical, eschatological. Ecclesiology (the study of the institutional church) is often academic, objective, ecumenical, and rather safe, protected as it is by institutions, and those deeply involved with them. But the denomination. Now, that is another story.

I regret to report that one of the recurring reactions I see among ministers toward their denominations is one of suspicion, fear, apathy, sometimes rejection, and occasionally antipathy. Unfortunately, it is often popular to criticize the denomination and its leaders. The "headquarters city" (it doesn't matter much whether it is Nashville, St. Louis, Springfield, Kansas City, or Anderson) is often the butt of sarcastic, even cruel jokes. Especially is this true, I think, among the younger, more naive ministers whose idealism relating to the Kingdom is being challenged by the realities of denominational life and practice.

The denomination elects persons to office, adopts resolutions addressed to controversial issues, and seeks to raise budgets from already overburdened congregations. And ministers sometimes experience feelings of disenchantment with it all. Then, the temptation is to distance oneself from the denomination, or just go independent. Sure, there are faults in any denomination. But the greater fault may be the spirit of independence, which nourishes an attitude which refuses to be accountable to anyone or any group.

My appeal, then, to any minister who is experiencing this sort of alienation, is simply this: let your attitudes be changed. These questions might help in this process:

1. What does the Bible say about unity and diversity?

2. What is there in my personality makeup that causes me to withhold trust of others?

3. Have I made it my business to get to know personally some of the agency executives and denominational leaders that I find myself set against?

4. Have I examined my denominational heritage with an appreciative view of its pioneers and purposes?

5. Can I honestly affirm the qualifications and commitment of my denominational leaders, and still objectively critique and constructively criticize their efforts?

6. Can I reaffirm my loyalty to my denominational group even though I may not always totally agree with its corporate decisions, nor with the statements made by its various spokespersons?

7. Am I willing to work for reform and renewal from *within* the group, rather than taking potshots from *outside*?

8. Am I wise enough to realize that there is strength in the group, and that together we can accomplish what we cannot do alone?

9. Am I humble enough to submit my ideas and plans to the scrutiny of others and benefit from their collected wisdom and discernment?

10. Am I courageous enough to reach out to others who may be sensing similar feelings of distance from the institutional church, in order to give and get guidance and support?

11. Have I made this a matter of prayer, confessing my own stubbornness, repenting of my envy, and seeking forgiveness for any damage I might have caused in my denomination?

The following sentence, fraught with sadness, pain, and danger, summarizes the issue of pastoral accountability in the free churches: *There is a general tendency among us for our clergy to be servants of all, but accountable to none.* The *sadness* of this Lone Ranger approach to ministry is that the church at large is denied the richness of collegial leadership. The *pain* of ministers who tend to be loners is that when they get caught in a squeeze they have no one to whom they can turn for help. The *danger* of an individualistic approach to ministry is the potential damage it can do to the church. The recent rumblings among the ordained television superstars provide a sad illustration of what happens when there is little or no accountability. And who can measure the damage to the church when such well publicized flaunting of authority occurs?

Broadening The Base Of Accountability

My concern for strengthening ecclesiastical connections represents an attempt to broaden the base of our spiritual accountability. Spiritual formation needs to be set in the broadest context possible. Perhaps I have left the impression that to present one's self for spiritual direction and accountability is a decision made rather whimsically by the individual, acting on private inner prompting. Of course, there is a sense in which to enter into intentional spiritual formation (especially the initiation of a spiritual friendship) is a very private matter, based upon the movement of the Spirit in one's life.

But spirituality is also a communal matter. As Christians, we are members of a Body, and responsible to it. As clergy, we belong to a professional fraternity. We owe it to our peers, our congregations, and our denominational group, to be growing, spiritually vital persons. Currently, there seems to be an increase of collegiality among pastors of many faith traditions, and this ecumenical spirit is cause for celebration. When ecumenism means cooperation, fellowshipping, and mutual appreciation, much can be gained. (When ecumenism means amalgamation, compromise and bland theology, count me out!)

It is in a mood of collegiality, honest sharing, and questing, that ministers can join together to build support networks that will include elements of accountability. And in this sort of environment, clusters of clergy and lay ministers can learn from each other, experience mutual support, and provide spiritual direction for one another. Perhaps denominational leaders need to take the initiative in order to build a sense of camaraderie among the clergy, and a sense of loyalty to the denomination.

A Case History

Consider the antithesis of this fraternal approach to ministry just described. Let me now provide a fictitious description of a pastor who is skillful, dynamic, personable, influential, and courageous. His congregation grows rapidly and they expand into radio, television, a book store, a nursing home, a school, numerous associates, an extensive building program, and so on. His energy seems to know no limits. What you have is a one-man dynamo — charismatic, successful, accountable to no one, vulnerable to no one, deeply known by no one. A powerful loner, running an expanding empire. But he doesn't really talk to anyone, and he doesn't really listen to anyone. And, he doesn't have time to pray. The years fly by. In a sense, he ''outgrows'' his denomination as his reputation expands.

What happens when stress and burnout begin to take their toll? He is getting a little older by now, and besides, he needs new frontiers to conquer. You already know how the story will develop, don't you? He begins to experience a lot of tiredness. He has a series of physical illnesses that linger. A major conflict in the church disrupts the harmony they've had for several years and the pastor gets discouraged. He tries harder and does more, but nothing much seems to work. Middlescence has set in, and minor illnesses nag him. The fun and the zest are mostly gone. Largely because of frustration, feelings of failure, and resentment that is probably unfocused, he becomes the victim of some kind of moral failure — a series of little ones or one big one — probably having to do with money, sex, or power. Now he is trapped. Where does he turn for help? He can't. He has appointed himself (unconsciously, of course) God's Prophet, and he can admit no wrong. Blame follows. Others are at fault, not him. And the fall of that man is miserable, and massive, and messy.

This made-up but realistic story need never happen — IF. *If* the busy pastor will take time to pray, to get to know himself/herself and God, build an adequate support network and use it, and then get help when adversity strikes, this story need not happen. Please understand that support networks are not only for the bad times. Accountability is not a virtue just when we are in trouble. Unless we learn to rely on others as well as the Lord, on an everyday basis as a lifestyle, we won't be able to seek and use help when disaster strikes. It is absolutely essential that leaders maintain close faith group connections.

The bottom line is, we really do need each other. Spirituality and ministry are corporate gifts. The wisdom of the Body is superior to our own. Whenever I find myself thinking or acting in opposition to the collected wisdom and discernment of my church, I need to inquire whether or not I am in error. I need to be sensible enough to accept the guidance of a spiritual director, to listen to the voice of congregational and denominational leaders, and to heed the counsel of wise elders. The spirituality and accountability of ministers is not just a concern of the individual. It is a concern of the whole church. Tend your denominational connections!

VI. If you wish to grow in voluntary spiritual accountability, develop some accountability covenants.

I think it helps to formalize intentions. So, I suggest that you carefully think through the several areas in which you wish to become more accountable, write out your intentions clearly, and then share them with the appropriate persons or groups. As starters, you may want to create a covenant with your spiritual friend. Then, you may seek to intentionalize your relationships with your congregation, your denomination, and your profession.

Covenant Of Spiritual Direction

In Chapter II, I described the process of spiritual direction, but I reserved for this chapter a discussion on creating an accountability covenant. To mutually develop a covenant is to make intentional and clear the basis upon which two persons will work together, one as spiritual director and the other as directee.

Let us assume that one has identified a potential director, met to discuss the possibilities, and mutually agreed to proceed.

Now it is their second session together, and the agenda is to discuss mutual needs and expectations with reference to the relationship. Decisions need to be made on several very specific issues. These decisions, reduced to writing, will guide future sessions and help prevent misunderstanding and frustration.

Agreements need to be reached in at least the following areas, and written down in your journal for future reference:

1. Meetings.
   (Dates, place, time, length of sessions)
2. Expectations.
   Based on understandings and previous experiences, what do each of you expect of the process?
3. Agenda.
   What are the responsibilities of each of you in the sessions? What will be the focus of the *next* meeting?
4. Accountability.
   What kind of guide will you provide for your director to use in calling you to account for your spiritual life? (See Appendix C for a sample guide.)
5. Evaluation.
   Periodically, the process needs to be critiqued. How are you doing? Are you both accomplishing your goals? Does the covenant need to be revised?

The directee needs to keep in mind that he/she is the initiator of the process, and is responsible to ask for what is desired from the relationship. In essence, a service (direction) is being sought from a resource person (director). Thus, the directee *asks* the director for some time; *describes* clearly what is needed; *invites* the director to call him/her to accountability; and *welcomes* honest evaluations of their work together. The objective remains growth in the Spirit.

Other Covenants

Inasmuch as Christians are covenant people, ministers are probably open to the whole idea of intentionalizing professional relationships by the use of covenants. I hope I am right! Let me, then, briefly mention three other forms that a covenant might take.

First, if you will refer to Appendix I, you will see a description of a "Covenant Between a Pastor and a Congregation." While the sample is very general and needs to be fleshed-out, it might provide a starter for the person wishing to prepare one. Additional information and guidance may be obtained by writing to appropriate denominational offices.

Second, if you will refer to Appendix J, you will see a sample "Code of Ethics." Do not simply accept this code, but prepare your own. Of course, feel free to use the sample as a starter, but you will need to personalize it to fit your own situation and commitments. The sample which is provided is one that I prepared while a seminary student in the sixties, and which, with minor revisions over the years, continues to express my convictions and ideals.

Third, if you will refer to Appendix K, you will see a sample "Job Description for a Minister in the Church of God." Again, this sample would need to be revised to fit your needs and your situation. My hope is that it will prompt some discussions between you and your congregation, and will nudge you in the direction of defining your ministerial identity. As with the Code of Ethics, I prepared this Job Description while I was a seminary student. On several occasions I used it as an aid to building a pastoral relationship with a congregation.

Conclusion

Recently I was reading in Brother Lawrence's little book, and I came across a delightful passage "on placing our sins between us and God." He made it sound so helpful that I've been trying it. I redefined "sins" to include fears, grudges, temptations, anger, ego, resentment, and so on. And then I wrote this meditation:

> *I give them up to you, God, Asking your sufficient grace. I've tried to handle them, My Father, and I cannot.*
>
> *I refuse to hide them behind me, O God, for I cannot.*
>
> *I quit trying to manage them alone, My God, for I cannot.*
>
> *I'll quit hoping they'll just go away, O Lord, for they will not.*
>
> *So, I place my sins between us, Knowing that what I cannot do, You, my God, Cannot refuse to do.*
>
> *And what I reluctantly admit and surrender, You gladly accept, And forgive, And redeem.*
>
> *Thank you, God, for redemption.*

This chapter on accountability really is about getting right with God, and being honest with others. God, grant us the grace!

There was a time (or it seems) when life was simpler, when we *knew* right from wrong, and when we understood what a sin was, and what the penalty was for it. We looked with confidence to our spiritual leaders and the Bible for answers and guidance and models. And it may be that some of us purchased a naive, secure, religious system, paid for with our own gullibility and conformity, resulting in a sort of perpetual spiritual adolescence.

But times have changed! We have seen a "graying" of our society, and now there are fewer either/or solutions to issues, and fewer questions can be answered with a simple yes or no. We have been encouraged to think for ourselves, work out our own salvation, celebrate our uniqueness, pull ourselves up by our own boot straps, and, even dialogue with God. Frankly, I find reason to rejoice in this humanizing process as long as it is subjected to the judgment of biblical principles.

And in these uncertain times, it is encouraging to note signs of a hunger for biblical authority, for Christian integrity, and for authentic witnesses. We are seeing a movement toward collegiality among the clergy. Multitudes of believers meet in small groups for prayer and mutual support. The Christian church finally seems to be taking seriously the idea of the priesthood of all believers — we are increasingly becoming ministers to each other.

Perhaps, as you read this chapter on accountability, you picked up a note of pessimism or criticism. Let's face it: We haven't done very well with voluntary accountability in the free churches. But I see many hopeful signs! Individualism in ministry has been tried and found wanting. Now I see an increasing number of clergy meeting with spiritual friends or colleague clusters for mutual discernment, nurture, and prayer. What I'm seeing may be the vanguard of a healthier, more effective profession. The word for today is accountability. And the spirit of it is love: love for God, for our calling, for our professional peers, for our faith community. Accountability can be terribly legalistic (having to do with counting, I suppose), unless we remember love.

V

Prayer

*... one of his disciples said to him, Lord teach us
to pray ... (Luke 11:1).*

The purpose of this chapter is to consider the *practice* of prayer. I will not attempt to address the various theories, definitions, forms and occasions of Christian prayer. Rather, I want to focus primarily on one type of prayer — personal prayer — that has as its goal the experiential knowledge of God. In personal prayer, we can build a relationship with our Lord, that will nourish our souls.

To write just one brief chapter on prayer and spiritual formation is a bit presumptuous, I suppose. But inasmuch as many useful volumes on prayer have already been written, I see no need for duplication here. What I hope to do is to discuss the practice of prayer, and share with you some of the ideas and methods that have been helpful to me and to others. So, let's consider ways of praying.

According to Henri Nouwen,

*We have fallen into the temptation of separating minis-
try from spirituality, service from prayer. Our demon*

115

<blockquote>says, 'We are too busy to pray; we have too many needs to attend to; too many people to respond to, too many wounds to heal. Prayer is a luxury, something to do during a free hour, a day away from work, or on a retreat. The few who are exclusively concerned with prayer — such as Trappists, Poor Clares, and some isolated hermits — are not really involved in ministry. They are set free for single-minded contemplation and leave Christian service to others.' But to think this way is harmful; harmful for ministers as well as for contemplatives. Service and prayer can never be separated (Nouwen, 1977, p. 12).</blockquote>

Prayer and ministry are inseparable. Praying may be the most important thing a minister *does*. This chapter will contain helps for the busy minister who desires a satisfying prayer life.

Effective praying requires certain attitudes.

1. We need a *longing* to experience the presence of God. To pray is to commune with God. To "practice the presence of God" is a way of living which recognizes that all of life is sacred, and we are intended for fellowship with God. Do you have a deep longing to sense that constant presence?

2. We need a *yearning* for the power of God. Are you sensitively aware of your deep need for God, and convinced of the possibilities available to us? Is "to be used of God" one of the goals of your life?

3. We need a *willingness* to obey God. To pray is to seek to fit our will and actions into Divine guidance. Are you willing to obey God, totally?

4. We need a *commitment* to the value of prayer. Do you believe in and trust the process? If your answer to each of these questions is "yes," you have a good attitude for prayer.

If you are "praying through" this book as I suggested in the Introduction, you may now want to reflect on the above paragraph before you proceed. Why not record some honest responses to the questions I have asked? Remember: reading, reflecting, praying, and writing provide a good formula for spiritual growth.

Let me continue to explore the idea of the right frame of mind for prayer. Prayer is your leap of faith into the greatness of God. Don't be overly concerned with dynamics, methods, or schedules. The important thing is to pray — to trust the Spirit and your own sanctified intuition. The best way to find God is to plunge with abandon into the great mercy and love of God.

The right frame of mind for prayer includes the recognition that prayer and the Word of God are inseparable. Prayer and Bible reading go together! In prayer, you speak; in the Word, God speaks. That is an over-simplification, but it suggests a mindset that is essential to a vital prayer life. Bible study needs to be guided by and empowered by prayer. Prayer needs to be informed by and nourished by Bible study.

There is a prior issue here, it seems to me. It has to do with one's trust in the integrity of scripture. Can you say, testimonially, and with all sincerity, that the Bible is true, that it is what it claims to be, that it is inspired and authoritative? If you can, the Bible for you will likely become God's Word of encouragement, nourishment, and direction. If you cannot, you will likely be forever subjecting it to scholarly analysis and intellectual examination, in search of "proofs" of its reliability.

Please understand that I am not making an appeal for a rejection of the scholarly approach to the Bible. As Christians, we need to be learned in all the critical methods of Bible study available to us. But there is a "beyondness" that is often neglected. Part of one's serious study of the Scriptures is the step of acceptance.

The Word was intended to be received. And that takes a faith assumption, or a leap of faith. *Beyond* the research, the analysis, the critical study — one comes to the place of choice. Shall I choose to believe, and then stake my life and ministry upon that conscious choice? Of course there still may be unresolved intellectual questions. But I exhort you to *choose* to believe in God's Word!

Such a faith declaration needs to be made within the context of study and information, not ignorance. Sadly, the element of childlike faith is sometimes neglected by the scholar. While being a serious student of the Bible is essential, one experientially needs to move "beyond" to the place where response and obedience are primary. The scholarship might be called "the schoolmaster" that leads one to the central concern of the Word — personal encounter with and loyalty to the God of the Bible.

So, the right frame of mind for prayer, as well as for Bible study, is an attitude of faith and trust. It is a matter of deciding to believe in spite of doubts. It is a matter of trusting the truth and authority of God's Word, even though intellectually, one still may have some unresolved questions. It is believing what one cannot prove!

I have indicated that methods or schedules are not fundamental to prayer. More important is the mind-set or attitude with which one prays. The main thing is to pray. Perhaps there is another way of saying what I'm getting at. The bottom line may be having a prayerful heart. How is that accomplished?

First, it is a gift of God. God places within us a desire to know and experience fellowship with Him. Second, we discipline our lives in order to create space and time for God in our hearts. That involves rejection of all evil that would hinder our communion. It is impossible to have a prayerful heart while living an un-Godly lifestyle. Third, we nurture our souls by adding the disciplines that contribute to growth in holiness.

The first draft of this chapter is being written while I am in residence in a house of prayer in Arizona. In a few days I shall go to another house of prayer in Texas, for a week or so. I trust that the beauty and peacefulness of this place will inspire me to write clearly and helpfully! It surely has provided a dynamic dimension to my own prayer life. Part of my current prayer pilgrimage involves reflection upon my own prayer practices, as well as learning some new ones. Please allow me to share in a rather personal way at this point.

For most of my life, prayer has been very active. I bombarded heaven, using urgent, sometimes almost hostile language to express my prayers to God. Prayer was a "labor," or "work." I "agonized" in prayer. At times I "held onto the horns of the altar," or "stormed the gates of heaven," or "wrestled in prayer." Occasionally I "claimed the victory" in advance. Mostly, I told God what I wanted, and gave instructions on how to meet my needs.

My purpose here is not to make a value judgment on the kind of praying that I did, for I believe that our merciful God hears all sincere prayers and there is a place for *active* praying. I only want to say that I have found a way to pray that is more meaningful to me. That new way simply means more listening and less talking, or *receptive* praying.

In the past, I felt that I wasn't praying unless I was talking to, instructing, reminding, or beseeching God for my own needs, or on behalf of others. I thought that I had to be active in order to accomplish certain objectives in prayer. But I have broadened my understanding of prayer. Now, I don't have to be speaking in order to be praying. I can sit quietly in meditation. Or, I can pray a few verses of Scripture. Or, I can just relax and enjoy God's presence in a chapel or on a mountain trail. With a greater variety of ways to pray, I find it easier to pray for longer periods of time. Personal prayer then, seeks a good balance of active (kataphatic) and receptive (apophatic) praying.

I hope that I don't lose credibility when I admit to being a beginner in prayer. Oh yes, I've prayed for as long as I can remember. But strangely, I was 50 years old when, in June of 1984, I experienced a significant breakthrough, and learned some important things about prayer. Furthermore, at that time, I really began to pray! Most of my life I made the excuse that I was too busy to spend time each day in prayer. (Usually, of course, I did an obligatory five minutes!) Now, I find that because I am busy, I must take some time with the Lord, and I do so. Prayer is becoming increasingly meaningful for me. I believe it can for you, too.

Words are inadequate for me to express my deep convictions about the centrality of prayer in the spiritual formation of ministers. That conviction emerged early in my ministry, perhaps more through frustration than fulfillment, in prayer. Now, after twenty years as a teacher of ministerial students, I am even more convinced. If beginning ministers learn theology and psychology and ecclesiology, but fail to learn to pray, the consequences will be sad indeed. I am trusting for a renewal in the professional ministry — a renewal born in prayer. I call for denominational officers, colleges, seminaries, and congregations everywhere to provide the instruction, the models, the motivation, and — yes, the time — so that leaders can become persons of prayer.

As we continue our consideration of the practice of prayer, I would like now to identify several ways of praying. I will not provide sophisticated justifications for using these approaches to prayer, but will depend upon you, the reader, with the guidance of the Holy Spirit, to select and utilize whatever seems most appropriate among these ideas.

The Lord's Prayer

The familiar "Our Father," often called the model prayer, was provided by Jesus to teach us, primarily, the attitude of prayer. Surely Jesus was more concerned with the spirit of our praying, than the particular words that were used. I believe that the frequent use of this familiar prayer enhances the liturgy of worshipping congregations, as well as the private devotions of individuals. I recommend its regular use, with the assurance that familiarity will not breed contempt, but appreciation.

In the prayer, (Matthew 6:9-13), Jesus instructed His disciples (and us) regarding the proper attitude of prayer. He taught us to pray in the following manner:
1. With a sense of community ("Our," v. 9)
2. With a sense of awe ("Father," v. 9)
3. With a sense of praise ("Hallowed," v. 9-10)

4. With a sense of need ("Give," v. 11-13)

5. With a sense of hope ("Kingdom," v. 13)

Note that the Lord's prayer alludes to the essential themes of a corporate worship service as well as a private prayer. The themes of community (church), praise to God, recognition of human need, and Christian hope, provide a balanced approach to God and a theologically complete liturgical formula. Therefore, we would do well to use this prayer frequently!

The Jesus Prayer

The Jesus Prayer is a brief, simple prayer that can be used in many ways in a variety of settings. Because it is simple and brief, yet true to the Gospel message, it is easily remembered, understood and repeated. It is generally believed to have originated in the sixth century, though it has roots in the New Testament (see Mark 10:47, Luke 17:13, 18:13, and 18:39). Especially popular in the Orthodox Church, it has been widely used throughout Christendom, and among persons of all ages. For a particularly beautiful description of how one can use this prayer to "pray without ceasing," see *The Way of a Pilgrim*, by an unknown nineteenth century Russian peasant (Image Books, 1978).

The Jesus Prayer, which says simply, "Lord, Jesus Christ, Son of God, have mercy on me, a sinner," helps to set the proper mental attitude toward prayer. A sincere repetition of the twelve words will lead persons to:

1. Acknowledge Jesus as Lord in their lives;

2. Recognize the Divinity and Kingship of Jesus;

3. Proclaim the relationship of Jesus and God;

4. Confess dependence upon God, and the need for forgiveness and reconciliation;

5. Personalize petitions; (The plural "us" may be substituted for the singular "me" when appropriate. Or, one may choose to insert the name of another person, in place of the "me," in order to pray petitionally.)

6. Approach God in humility; (To remember that we are human is both realistic and therapeutic.)

The Jesus Prayer may be found in other forms, that is, with slightly different wording (e.g. "Lord Jesus Christ, have mercy on me"). I see nothing wrong with one making alterations upon it, if that will increase its effectiveness for the user. For example, one might abbreviate the prayer to an even simpler, "Lord, have mercy." Many people find that the repetition of the single word "Jesus," provides a powerful prayer.

Long before I heard of the Jesus Prayer, I used "Jesus is Lord! Lord have mercy," as a preface to private prayer and as a device for centering down as I began my devotional time. I often use the phrase, repeated over and over silently, in order to help me relax physically. I say silently, "Jesus is Lord," as I breath in. Then I say "Lord have mercy," as I breathe out. The content of the prayer reminds me of my commitment to and my relationship with God. Its use provides an approach to prayer that is simple, adaptable, and transportable.

Some may object to using the Jesus Prayer in this manner on the grounds that the content of the prayer seems to focus excessively on the negative ("Have mercy on me, a sinner") rather than on positive themes such as peace, hope, and joy. To that objection I would reply that the critique is valid, but we really do need to be reminded of the human tendency toward pride. I think it is obvious to all how much the spirit of our age is self-absorption and self-aggrandizement. In the face of widespread egoism, even among believers, we need to be confronted with the reality of our humanity. To ask for mercy is a cleansing and healing practice, even for the born-again Christian.

Others may object to the Jesus Prayer on the grounds that it is repetitious, simplistic, and surely must be an insult to the intelligence of God and the pray-er. To which I reply, perhaps it is all of the above, if it is said with the wrong attitude. But if it is repeated in a manner that is honestly prayerful, such use of the familiar can serve to draw us quickly and powerfully into the presence of God. In this case, the sincere attitude sanctifies the method. Anytime that we can eliminate form and methodological distractions in worship, we have enhanced the experience. So, the simple is advantageous. And repetition serves to focus.

What are some ways that one might use the Jesus Prayer? The Jesus Prayer may be helpful in the following ways as one seeks to develop the prayerful heart, and thus, be able to "pray without ceasing."

1. It helps from the *physical* perspective. When beginning to pray, I often start breathing slowly and deeply while repeating the prayer a dozen or so times. This is an excellent means of relaxing the mind and body. Whenever I sense tension in my body (such as before preaching, or between appointments) such a regimen helps relieve the tightness that often works against effectiveness. Our bodies need these quiet moments in order to recover from the stresses of hectic living. So, prayer is an aid to physical health!

2. The Jesus Prayer is helpful from the *mental* perspective. It provides a focus for centering. Others use mandalas or mantras with similar results. But for me, the Jesus Prayer moves me more immediately to the object and focus of my prayer. To center on my relationship with the Lord, is to dispel other distractions to prayer. I am thus enabled, to a degree, to control my thoughts, and subject them to the discipline of my will.

3. Finally, the Jesus Prayer is helpful to me from the *spiritual* perspective. It aids in positioning the heart toward honor, praise, confession, and supplication. When I begin to pray with the attitude of reverence, repentance, and humility, I am spiritually ready to encounter God, express my needs, and make intercessions. Thus the Jesus Prayer helps prepare for prayer and to continue praying. Because it contains a brief but powerful credo, it serves as a theologically whole affirmation of faith. This adds intellectual integrity to the devotional practice.

Meditation

The word meditate means to muse over, to ponder, to consider. Christian meditation involves paying careful attention to our internal spiritual processes, as well as listening for the voice of God. To meditate, we need to separate ourselves *from* the busyness, noise, and pressure of our world, and separate ourselves *to* the quiet, healing encounter with God. This takes time and effort and waiting. The Psalmist said that the "blessed" man takes his delight in the Lord and meditates upon Him day and night (Psalm 1:2). Again, the Psalmist said, "I think of thee upon my bed, and meditate on thee in the watches of the night" (Psalm 63:6).

It is helpful to have a place of quiet to which one can go regularly for times of meditation. The discipline of a structured "meeting" with God, will produce positive results in the life of the believer. The "meeting" proceeds on four levels: the *cognitive*, suggesting that there are some beliefs, traditions, learning that are involved; the *relational*, suggesting that a person and a personal God encounter each other; the *affective*, suggesting that there are experiences and feelings involved; the *missional*, suggesting there is a horizontal dimension of service and witness.

Perhaps more essential than the development of disciplined patterns of meditation is the development of a prayerful heart. Without a doubt, the prayerful heart is the outgrowth of months or years of meditational experimentation, persistence, and appeals for mercy. Ideally, one's walk with God becomes so central and continuous that contact with the Divine seems unbroken throughout the day. One's heart is constantly in tune with God. Idealistic? Perhaps. But the image described is better than the opposite, which is a periodic, frantic, spiritual refill during crisis times.

Meditation, then, may be defined as an exercise in inner quieting, centering down, listening, waiting. Prayer, on the other hand, may be generally understood as requests, supplication, seeking change, learning, surrendering, committing —

in other words, more active, whereas meditation is more receptive.

How does the busy minister arrange for this regular quiet time? By making it a priority! It won't do much good to yearn for a retreat in the mountains, or to wish that the phone would quit ringing. Over-scheduled ministers will need to learn to create contemplative moments in the midst of pressure. I think it was Susannah Wesley, mother of nineteen children, who pulled her apron over her head when she wanted to pray. Some of us may need to learn to say no (without feeling guilty) and let the phone go unanswered (or get an answering machine). Dare we discipline our urge to rush on in service to others in order to meet our appointment with God? Can we be still and *know* God?

Getting Started

Some people have the marvelous ability to concentrate. They seem to be able to ignore the distractions, focus their attention, and manage their time in order to grow in the Christian disciplines. Others are driven willy-nilly from idea to idea and plan to plan. When pausing to pray, thoughts, plans, schedules, and fantasies dance through their heads. A half hour is set aside for prayer, and instead, a cacophony of voices from inside and outside beg to be heard. Is it easy or difficult for you to concentrate on praying?

In either case, most of us long for the leisure and solitude that aids personal prayer. We may differ in the specifics of that longing, but when pandemonium is more characteristic of our day than prayer, our hearts generally yearn for peace.

I am assuming that most readers of this book are busy people. I wish that I had some instant formulas that would insure "success" in prayer. But there is no magic when it comes to the deeper life. It takes time and patience, effort and grace. But because we do live with a lot of tension, bombarded with stimuli of many kinds, we need to find some simple, workable methods of prayer. Some of the "methods" may be nothing more than routines, or habits that we follow, as we seek to experience God in prayer.

Carl Whitaker, in speaking of family therapy, said that the first and most continuing issue is the battle for structure. "When do we meet? Where? Who is in charge? Who has the power? How shall we do therapy? What is our contract?" So, too, in prayer, the basic questions are when, where, and how? The development of routines, or the formation of habits, help to address those basic questions.

Two initial obstacles to a vital prayer life have to do with *time* and *place*. The tendency is to think in terms of hours of uninterrupted prayer in a beautiful place of solitude. That may be an occasional possibility for most of us, but not very practical. However, we can consider moments, stop signs, and flowers.

Most of us can grab a moment here and there in order to turn our hearts toward God. These moments are not substitutes for an authentic "meeting" with God (daily, perhaps 20-30 minutes). Rather, they support the "meetings." These moments might be called "practicing the presence," and will help move us toward the development of a prayerful heart, as we seek to "pray without ceasing."

Opportunities for moments with God present themselves regularly. Why not let a stop sign or a traffic light be a reminder to pray? Or a flower suddenly discovered, can be a beautiful invitation to prayer. Prayer doesn't have to take place in a chapel, or beside a lake. It can happen when we're walking, riding, showering, or waiting. God provides many serendipitous opportunities. The thing is to claim the moments, enjoy the red lights, and look for more flowers!

Let us consider now the "how" question. What system do we use? Obviously, there are many options, and each person will need to develop his or her own style of praying. However, let me share mine, with the hope that it may contain some helpful ideas. In the description that follows, I am assuming a

30-minute block of time for prayer. If one is just beginning a disciplined prayer life, the suggested times may need to be shortened.

Phase I (About 10 Minutes)

I find that my first task as I begin praying is to center down. Usually, I have my prayer time immediately upon arriving at my office, shortly after 8 a.m. At other times, I use part of the noon hour for this purpose. In either case, I struggle to eliminate the distractions (the schedule for the day, things that need to be done) and focus upon God. I begin by relaxing my mind and body. I may do a few light stretching exercises (especially at noon), then, sitting comfortably, I breathe deeply, using a variation of the Jesus Prayer. I sit with eyes closed, repeating over and over, (as I breathe in) "Jesus is Lord!" (and as I breathe out), "Lord have mercy." I then pray a prayer of invocation (sometimes aloud) inviting God's presence, and opening myself to Him. I often use the "palms down, palms up" method at this point (see below).

Phase II (About 10 Minutes)

A second phase involves reading a brief passage of Scripture (often Psalms, Proverbs or John). Frequently I use the reading for the day from the devotional book which I keep with me (Job and Shawchuck, *A Guide to Prayer for Ministers and Other Servants*). It contains Scripture and readings based on the daily lectionary. I often make brief notes in my journal, when these readings speak helpfully to me. I resist the temptation to do serious Bible study at this point (commentaries, dictionaries, concordances, and so on), but discipline myself to stay in the devotional (right brain) mind-set. Frequently, I engage in what is called "Praying the Scriptures" (see p. 129).

Phase III (About 10 Minutes)

Generally, from this brief study, one word seems to be impressed upon me. I reflect on that word in a meditative way (relaxed, eyes closed) for a minute or so, repeating it silently. It becomes my "word for the day" (see below). Following that, I enter into a time of active prayer, using the ACTS model (see below). My journal is a helpful reminder of answered prayers, concerns and persons I'm praying for, and personal needs to be mentioned. So, I keep the journal handy. Occasionally, a kind schedule allows me a little more time, and sometimes I have a little less. In either case, I'm aware that I serve a patient God who is rich in mercy.

Palms Down, Palms Up

The "palms down, palms up" method I learned from Richard Foster in *Celebration of Discipline*. While seated comfortably and relaxed, in an attitude of prayer, hold your hands out in front of you, palms down. This symbolizes release, turning your needs, anxieties, fears, and concerns over to God. You are not holding onto, nor insisting on anything. Your attitude is one of conscious surrender. After a few minutes in this posture, turn your palms up. This symbolizes receptivity and acceptance. The attitude is, "What would you tell me Lord?" or "What would you provide for me?" This is not the time to ask for anything, but to wait in silence to receive. After developing a degree of comfort and skill with this device, you may find that it quickly helps you to "center down," as you begin to pray.

Word For The Day

The "word for the day" method is this: when reading a passage of Scripture *devotionally*, stay alert to the idea or message that has particular meaning for you on that occasion. At times, it may be the rather obvious key word in the passage. At other times, it may lie hidden, and will be discovered only by the seeking heart. In either case, it is the word that strikes a responsive chord, and one is drawn to meditate upon it. This word, impressed upon the mind and heart in prayer, will be recalled periodically during the day. It is amazing how often that word becomes the word of inspiration, encouragement, or instruction, which is needed later on in the day.

Acts Model Of Praying

The "ACTS Model" for prayer is this: the four letters, as an acrostic, provide a sequence for praying, that may be useful in private or public prayers.

Adoration. To give praise and honor to the triune God.

Confession. To acknowledge one's humanity and sense of need for forgiveness for all failure. (An examination of conscience, as John Wesley taught, is a helpful method of confession.)

Thanksgiving. To offer up sincere gratitude to the benevolent God of grace.

Supplication. To offer prayers of petition primarily for ourselves, and prayers of intercession, primarily for others.

Praying The Scriptures

Praying the Scriptures provides a method of joining devotional Bible reading to the practice of prayer. And I strongly believe that the two should not be separated. For a fuller treatment of this subject, see Maureen Gallagher, et al, *Praying with Scripture* (Paulist Press, 1983).

Let me, in summary fashion, offer some suggestions for practicing this method of prayer.

1. Begin by accepting the devotional approach to Scripture as valid for the believer seeking to know God *experientially*. (It is also valid to seek to know God from the intellectual perspective, so we engage in a quest for *understanding* (information, logic, proofs). But the end of that quest *could* be that one knows *about* God, but doesn't know God!) Therefore, in praying the Scriptures, one needs consciously to shift gears away from the intellectual (deductive) study of the Bible, to the more experiential, (inductive) personalized reading of it.

2. Find the time and place that will be relatively free from interruptions. Relax, and begin centering down. Find your passage of Scripture and read through it for the first time. Invite God's presence and illumination.

3. Let your attitude toward the passage be somewhat as follows:

   a. God is waiting to speak to me through the Word.
   b. God knows and cares about me and my concerns.
   c. The Bible has untold riches (insight, guidance, inspiration) that address me and my needs.
   d. The person I am at this moment has never experienced what this passage might be saying to me now.
   e. I *need* to listen to God. I *will* listen to God, as I explore, seek, and wait. I will obey God's guidance, as I understand it.

4. Experience the passage as fully as you can.

   a. Put yourself into the passage. Become a part of the scene or the story. Become one of the characters, or an observer of what is happening.
   b. Look at the other people in the passage. What do their faces, words, actions tell you?
   c. What is the underlying message from God, or the eternal truth in the passage?

d. What sounds do you hear? What do you see? What can you touch, and what touches you?

e. What are you feeling inside?

f. Talk with God. Tell God about your feelings, needs, hopes, complaints, and victories, which may relate to the passage. Then listen. What do you think God would say to you? What might other persons mentioned in the passage say to you and your situation?

5. Continue reading a few words or a verse at a time, talking with God about whatever you are prompted to share, and writing in your journal. Journal entries may include some or all of the following: a. *Insights* which provide guidance for living; b. *Inspiration* which provides courage and hope; c. *Themes* for further study and prayer; d. *Reminders* to act and pray on behalf of others. The journal, then, becomes a record of what one experiences during prayer and what one's intentions are as a result of praying.

6. The Bible is meant to be responded to. Therefore, it is appropriate to conclude a time of praying the Scriptures by asking such questions as: How, then, ought I to live? How might I share this good news with others? In what ways will I become involved in issues of righteousness, justice, and peace in my world?

While spending time with God needs no further rationale than cultivating the relationship, addressing the above questions do help provide a missional outlet that is both our mandate and deep spiritual need.

Walter Brueggemann says, "Praying the Psalms depends upon two things: 1) What we find when we come to the Psalms that is already there; and 2) What we bring to the Psalms out of our own lives" (Brueggemann, 1982, p. 27).

Thus, praying the Scriptures becomes an exercise in bringing these two realities together — the Divine address of God in Scripture, and human experience. This encounter represents one's struggle to understand the Bible, and make sense out of life. Prayers that result from this interaction provide insight, direction, and nurture — growth in Christ.

131

Journaling

To keep a journal is to add a dimension of discipline to one's prayer life that no other method will add. While some persons find journaling to be a very natural exercise, and thus, easier to do, all persons would benefit from the effort. One's journal must, in the final analysis, be one's own. Therefore, it is not appropriate for me to make a list of what a journal should contain. One's journal should be whatever one wants it to be.

George F. Simons says,

> *Each person's journal will have a mood of its own — certain predominant themes with variations and improvisations. Some will use the journal as a place to privately celebrate the wonder and loveliness of life. Others will make it a record of dreams and fantasies, or a workshop of experience. Some are books of inner searching and prayer (Simons, 1978, pp. 37-38).*

While I am reluctant to be definitive about the contents of a journal, I am willing to make a few suggestions about the process. Elaborate explanations are probably unnecessary. Like learning to swim, the best way to learn journaling is to jump in — with some basic helps nearby, of course. Now, let us consider three basic questions:

When does one write in a journal?

In the beginning, when one is developing the skill and habit, it is probably good to write every day. It may be nothing more than an entry giving the date, place, and time, with a sentence like "not much happening today." But the discipline of facing a blank page is a good one. At least it invites reflection and other spiritual exercises. It is a reminder that "I have an appointment with God." Some days, there will be a need to write, and the words will flow from your heart to the page. Occasionally, insight will break in to you and beg to be recorded. The tough part is making oneself physically, and mentally available to interact with one's deepest self, with devotional reading, and with God, in meditation. Then, the journal becomes a record of the interaction, and in many cases will help to facilitate it.

Likely, for most persons, there will be particularly busy times when no entries are made for several days. An attempt to "catch up" would be a laborious process. At that point, one might simply reflect upon the days since the last entry, and summarize, or write "headlines" (as in a newspaper) of the significant events or spiritual experiences. Thus, a few sentences may cover several days, and maintain the continuity of the journal. As a rule, though, it is better to record experiences soon after their occurrence.

Often, people ask, "Should I write when things are going bad for me, or just write about the positive experiences?" My answer is "both!" Of course, most of us are reluctant for others to know about our "down" times — especially the painful and sometimes ugly details. For that reason, the journal writer may want to take steps to assure that others do not have access to the writing. Or, better yet, in my opinion, one may simply decide that "this journal is me, warts and all, and I'll just not be bothered by the fact that someone, someday, may read it." This attitude of freedom and honesty allows for a fuller expression of who we are, including our struggles, and affords an opportunity for catharsis through the journal.

How much does one write?

A practical answer is: Write as much as you can without it becoming a chore. Try to make notes about the movement of the Spirit in your life, prayer themes, spiritual insights, goals and plans, and inner experiences. But don't write so much that it becomes wearisome, and you dread doing it. Often, a brief sentence can summarize a complex experience, or a word can prompt the remembering of a feeling or an idea. One may even develop one's own form of "shorthand" in order to reduce the amount written. Personally, my journal is an 8-1/2 x 11 spiral-bound notebook that costs $.69. I find that one this size lasts several months, it's economical, and if I ever misplace one, the loss is not substantial. They are beginning to accumulate now, so the date of use on the outside cover, helps me recover material when needed.

Why keep a journal?

There are witnesses in abundance that testify to the value of journal-keeping. From antiquity to the present, persons have kept journals or diaries, many of which have been published, thus passing the benefits along to others. For a more elaborate discussion of journaling, see the books listed in the bibliography by Simons and Klug.

Understandably, one keeps a journal for the same reason that one practices other spiritual disciplines, namely, for the enhancement of one's spiritual formation. Or, put another way, it is a method for the deepening and enriching of the life in Christ. For the person hungering after God, the journal provides a means for asking questions and recording answers; for clarifying issues and problems; for putting into permanent form those serendipity moments that come to us; for making a record of our progressive growth toward wholeness. And there are many other reasons, depending upon the needs and the hopes of the individual.

Richard Foster says that, "our Adversary majors in three things: noise, hurry, and crowds. If he can keep us engaged in 'muchness' and 'manyness', he will be satisfied" (Foster, 1978, p. 13). To approach a journal, with the proper attitude, is to allow ourselves a little time for listening to our inner selves, to hear the quiet voice of God, and to reflect on the meaning and purpose of our existence. Are you ready to experiment with this method of spiritual formation? If so, I suggest that you give it a six-month trial. And as you write faithfully, do some reading from the journals of others, such as Woolman, Wesley, and Nouwen.

Meetings

Are you sensing a need to take up a more disciplined

approach to personal prayer? If so, consider these simple suggestions for your regular "meetings" with God.

1. Don't begin this effort until there is first a yearning in your soul. Otherwise, it would be mechanical and you would find little satisfaction in prayer that was forced.

2. But if you are convinced that personal prayer is a worthwhile undertaking, and you sense the Spirit leading you to enter into it, do not be distracted nor delayed any longer.

3. Start out with the attitude, "Lord, teach us to pray" (Luke 11:1), and lean upon the guidance of the Spirit. As a learner, you need not expect perfection as you seek to grow in prayer.

4. Find a private place relatively free from distractions, set a time that can be kept faithfully, get comfortable, anticipate a meeting with God.

5. Consider the following five-step plan. You may want to plan on only five minutes at first. Don't push yourself too fast. After several months of regular "meetings," you may find that 15 or 20 minutes are hardly enough.

    a) Relax. Center down (use the Jesus Prayer, or your version of it). Pray for guidance.

    b) Read a brief Scriptural or devotional selection.

    c) Reflect. Identify your "word for the day."

    d) Pray. Try the ACTS method.

    e) Write in your journal.

6. When you conclude your "meeting," go in a sense of assurance, hope, and confidence. Make an appointment for the next meeting, and keep it. You will find that God will be there waiting! And by all means, be gentle with yourself.

A Perspective On Personal Prayer

At the beginning of one of the Byzantine liturgies, when the preliminary preparations are completed, and all is ready for the start of the Eucharist, the deacon approaches the priest and says, "It is time for the Lord to act." Such is the proper attitude of the believer, not only during corporate worship, but also in private prayer.

An understanding that the Lord is about to act, reminds us that personal prayer is not so much something which we initiate and do, as it is something which we share with God. True inner prayer is a time to remember that God is at work within us (Galatians 2:20) and that our responsibility is to be present for an encounter.

I exhort you, do not try to reach God only with the intellect — you will never know enough. Do not try to reach God only by climbing a ladder of good deeds — you will never accomplish enough. Do not try to reach God only through feelings — they are too fickle. Rather, try to reach God through prayer, for prayer is the language of the soul in communion with God. God has abundantly provided us all with love. So, pray in love, if you want to know God.

Nothing quite describes one's relationship with God like one's prayer life. We *are* what we pray! Our prayer life is a reflection of our souls. No wonder that it is essential that we "pray without ceasing" (1 Thessalonians 5:17).

There are many ways to pray, and each person must find his or her own style and methods. However, there do seem to be some basic patterns that are common among those persons who are effective in prayer. Henri Nouwen says that there are three "rules" which are always observed by such people:

> *... a contemplative reading of the word of God, a silent listening to the voice of God, and a trusting obedience to a spiritual guide. Without the Bible, without silent time, and without someone to direct us, finding our own way to God is very hard and practically impossible (Nouwen, 1975, p. 96).*

While I totally agree with Nouwen's three "rules" in principle, I would like to reframe his third rule to identify the Holy Spirit as the ultimate Guide of all of us. And in reference to a human guide, I would like to change the word "obedience" to "relationship." The idea of a *trusting relationship* with another believer who functions as a spiritual friend and guide, is more in keeping with my understandings of human personality and the Christian faith. "Obedience" to a person suggests the loss of Christian liberty.

Nouwen's emphasis upon Bible reading and solitude contains a message that needs to be heard. The spirit of our age is to analyze, or debate, or debunk the Scriptures, especially those parts which report miraculous events. Frequently we try to explain the mysteries of our faith, and in the process we often trivialize the transcendent.

To pray is to recover our innocence and become again as little children (Matthew 10:15). To pray is to open the impossibilities of human existence to the possibilities of an omnipotent God. I often heard Dr. Blackwelder say to his seminary students: "I believe it but I can't explain it." Prayer believes what is sometimes difficult to explain.

Another attitude about prayer is found in the beatitudes. Jesus said, "Blessed are the poor in spirit, for theirs is the kingdom of heaven" (Matthew 5:3). To be poor in spirit is to be aware of one's interior poverty, and to freely admit to a lack at the deepest level. That which is lacking is God. Whenever God is missing, self rushes in to fill the void.

So we find ourselves preoccupied with self (our own failures, fears, hurts, dependencies, frustrations, disappointments, sin) and with little energy or inclination to focus on God. And we get further into our poverty. But in a paradoxical way, Jesus said that those who are conscious of their poverty, can begin to seek the riches of God. In fact, the whole kingdom — everything — is available to them! This, I think, is the true spirit of prayer.

For the person who would grow in prayer, certain bad notions about prayer need to be dispelled.

1. Prayer is bombardment.

Well-meaning persons sometimes engage in storming the gates of heaven, travailing in prayer, and holding onto the horns of the altar. But it seems to me such prayers may be too demanding, a bit arrogant, and sometimes hostile.

2. Prayer is asking.

Too often we equate prayer with requests. We do too much "give me" praying, I fear. Sometimes we "claim the answer" in advance, without waiting to discern the will of the Lord. Occasionally we presume to know God's will, and claim "total victory" — which often is synonymous with whatever we are asking for. All too often, our asking has to do with our own health, wealth, and happiness.

3. Prayer is for the desperate.

As the saying goes, "There are no atheists in fox holes." So, prayer is for those who are dying, or who are afraid they are, or else they are in a crisis situation, like an airplane about to crash. Some people think that prayer is for weak, dependent types. As a last resort, see if God might help.

Obviously, these are inadequate notions about prayer. For some better notions about prayer consider the following:

1. Prayer is more fellowshiping with, than beseeching God.

2. Prayer is more listening to, than it is talking to God.

3. Prayer is more preparation to accept God's will, than it is influencing God to provide what we want.

4. Prayer is more a relationship or a life, than it is a series of pious acts.

Conclusion

In the midst of an American culture that values glitter, hurry, noise, and crowds, it will be difficult to swim against the stream as a contemplative. It is easy, as ministers, to go with the flow and get caught up in church programming that is based on "bigger is better."

As an antidote to our pell-mell lifestyles, that often results in spiritual impoverishment, burnout, or even breakdown, we need to discover a desert. If Jesus, and the early fathers, and the great saints went to the desert periodically, shouldn't we?

It is not a question of transporting oneself physically to a desert. Rather, it means creating a desert space in one's own heart. It means seeking constantly to find some time away from the crowds and the pressures in order to commune with God. It may mean only the closing of a door, or remaining awhile in an empty church building, or driving out into the country for a walk along a lonely lane. Finding a desert implies getting away from the "world," but perhaps more importantly, it implies devoting oneself fully, with fewer distractions, to God!

Let me sound this one word of warning: Avoid getting under some kind of bondage or guilt about prayer. There is a temptation to try to learn to pray like someone suggested you should, or like the great saints you have read about. Most of us have enough other causes for guilt without adding our prayer life to the list! Give yourself permission to be a learner, to fail sometimes in your efforts at prayer. Don't try so hard to do it yourself. Let the Spirit pray through you. Remember that prayer is one of God's gifts to you.

If the spiritual life of the minister is the integrating center for ministry, as I believe it is, then prayer is the core of the spiritual life. Therefore, prayer becomes the very heart and soul (the center) of ministry. It puts ministry "together" and provides wholeness. It also helps put the minister "together"! Prayer is the most important thing leaders *do*.

In this chapter I have written about "personal prayer." But there may be no such thing as "personal" prayer. Rather, there is a great cloud of witnesses who accompany us in this discipline. Saints gone on and saints in offices, farms, and factories pray with us in many languages and in many ways. We do not pray alone! Let us celebrate our participation in a community of praying people.

VI

Community

> *And let the peace of Christ rule in your hearts, to which indeed you were called in the one body. And be thankful. Let the word of Christ dwell in you richly, as you teach and admonish one another in all wisdom, and as you sing psalms and hymns and spiritual songs with thankfulness in your hearts to God (Colossians 3:15-16).*

This final chapter will define the context in which spiritual formation best takes place. Much of what has been said in previous chapters referred to the lonely struggle to pray and the need for solitude. No one can make the journey to Christ for us.

Dietrich Bonhoeffer expressed this paradox clearly when he said, "Let him who cannot be alone beware of community ... But the reverse is also true: Let him who is not in community beware of being alone." He also quoted Martin Luther, who said, "If I die, then I am not alone in death; if I suffer, they (the fellowship) suffer with me" (Bonhoeffer, 1954, p. 77).

This understanding of the Body of Christ is essential if the church is to succeed in bringing a measure of wholeness to a society that is fragmented, alienated, and selfish. Unless congregations become communities in the full sense, we will not be the church for which Christ died.

This chapter is not so much a discussion *about* the church as it is a message *to* the church. I hope that congregational leaders will engage in serious discussion of the issues raised, and then risk some programmatic changes and innovations. The questions that will guide our thinking are: What does our congregation believe about spiritual formation? How can we assist persons seeking to grow in spiritual depth? Is our congregation truly a community?

I will identify what I see as needs and then suggest ways that a congregation might help persons to grow in spirituality.

I. Believers need to clarify their concept of the church.

There is a continuing need to clarify our theological understandings of the church. We too often conceptualize it as an organization rather than a dynamic organism which it truly is. We too often think of it as an institution, rather than the Body as Paul described it. We even refer to the church as a building or a denomination. For many persons, church is a place we "go to," rather than a force that "goes." We too often view the church as a place of activities and action, rather than a fellowship for the purpose of becoming.

Elizabeth O'Connor helps us to rethink our concept of the church when she says,

> *We are not called primarily to create new structures for the church in this age; we are not called primarily to a program of service, or to dream dreams or have visions. We are called first of all to belong to Jesus Christ as Savior and Lord, and to keep our lives warmed at the hearth of His life. It is there the fire will be lit which will create new structures and programs of service that will draw others into the circle to dream and have visions.*

> *To understand this is to be thrown back upon those disciplines which are the only known gateways to the grace of God; for how do we fulfill the command to love,*

Congregations that focus more upon integrity than increase in numbers, will likely be growing spiritually. When will we trade our success mentality for servanthood? I have observed congregations become whirling dervishes of activities, programs, and "ministries." Their assumption is, I suppose, that the unconverted want to become part of another frantically active organization and that the already converted need to stay busy. Of course, I don't mean to encourage lethargic congregations. But activity and spirituality simply are not synonymous.

More important than what a congregation *does* is who the congregation *is*. What about the quality of life of the parishioners? Do the people have time to pray or are they too busy with church and other activities? Jerry Cook's book *Love, Acceptance and Forgiveness*, is a case study of a congregation that took seriously its calling and mission. It focused more on ministry and less on activity, but it grew in numbers. It didn't talk much about denominational distinctiveness or church discipline, but it lived a theology of forgiveness and love. And people sought it out.

II. Believers need help with the issue of balancing the individual and communal elements of faith and practice.

Prior to the 1960s, evangelical Christians tended to accept the decisions of their leaders, the authority of the Scriptures, and the traditional practices of the church. Typically, believers were willing to sacrifice personal accomplishments for the good of others or the church. Vocations were held in high esteem.

However, during the sixties and seventies, there was a focus upon "me" and "now." Personal fulfillment became the objective. Exaltation of the individual became the norm. The death of God and a decline in church memberships reflected an eroding religious authority. Persons inside and outside the church spoke more in terms of conscience than authority and obedience. Believers favored the "spirit" over the "law," and so anything "charismatic" was in.

Now, in the nineties, we are trying to bring balance and harmony. We dare not lose the value of personhood that was highlighted during the sixties and seventies, but we need to remember the importance of community. In terms of spirituality we need a balance that allows both the valid functioning of conscience and individual liberty plus a relational, connected authority and accountability to the Body of Christ.

Unfortunately, spiritual formation has been given bad press by the misinformed (based on limited exposure or poor models) who characterize spirituality in terms of private piety and monastic tendencies. While true spirituality includes some individual aspects, there is more to it than just that. Congregations need the teaching and modeling of a spirituality that offers significant personal growth opportunities, while being solidly rooted in the Christian tradition, and maintaining close connections with the church at large.

III. Believers need help in valuing the differences within the congregation.

Differences are threatening, but uniformity is deadening. While we are created in the Divine image, God is wonderfully diverse. The remarkable diversity within the human race must surely have been intentional. The challenge before us is not only to tolerate the differences but to cherish them.

Take a good look at your congregation. How many physical types, leadership styles, theological orientations, economic backgrounds, personality types, and so on, are represented? Many! The miracle is that congregations manage to hang together.

I suppose the place to begin is to get out the message that human beings are unique. That means we are not alike and never will be! And any theological position that demands uniformity needs to be re-considered. The message that differences are acceptable will not be received unanimously. There is a powerful human urge to squeeze others into our own mold. But the message must be emphasized: Every member of the Body has a valued function. Our variety is our strength.

The Bible provides us with a theology of diversity. Recent psychological insights into personality differences give us practical handles for identifying and understanding personality differences. Carl Jung' studies in typology have been especially helpful in understanding and utilizing human differences.

Congregations might benefit from using the Myers-Briggs Type Inventory, especially among church leaders, to help discover personality types, preferences, and relationship patterns. (See Appendix D for a brief discussion of the MBTI and ministry.)

I believe that people have a higher level of toleration for that which they understand. An easily-administered test like the MBTI might serve to de-mystify personality differences and move persons to a greater appreciation of those differences. When persons cherish the differences in the congregation, they will be able to work together, strengths and gifts can be utilized, and the disharmony caused by misunderstandings can be reduced.

Discrimination

Not only do congregations need help with theological and personality differences, they also need to address sexual, racial, and age differences. We have only recently become aware of just how sexist, racist, and ageist the church is. Of course, awareness is only the first step — and certainly, not everyone is even aware. But growth in these areas is needed if all of the congregation is to experience holistic spiritual health.

Discrimination based on sex is unacceptable to Christian people. It is not acceptable for congregations to treat women or men unfairly when it comes to employment and advancement. To reserve leadership to men only is not tolerable.

The cheap, degrading jokes about women *and* men ought not be part of Christian conversations. There is no excuse for blatantly sexist language. We really do need to acknowledge that 51 percent of the population is "she," and "he" doesn't include them at all. A congregation cannot experience holistic spiritual health as long as sexist practices prevail.

Discrimination based on race is unacceptable to Christian people. It is no longer tolerable to view any race as inferior. Nor can congregations refuse to serve persons simply because of skin color or national origins. Until we can reach our hand in fellowship to every blood-washed one, we have not become one in the bond of love that we sing about. A congregation cannot experience holistic spiritual health as long as racist practices prevail.

Discrimination based on age is unacceptable to Christian people. We need to recognize the increasing number of older persons among us as a gift from God. These elders provide a rich resource for community life. Can we provide ways for them to become mentors and enablers of others, as they gradually relinquish active leadership in the congregation? Can their insights and influence still be useful in the congregation as their energy for activity wanes? A congregation cannot experience holistic spiritual health as long as ageist practices prevail.

We dare not, by our thoughtlessly discriminatory practices and language cause certain members of the Body to feel unneeded and unwanted. We may need to reach out again and again in order to touch those who for many years have felt rejected simply because of age, sex, or race. Sensitive congregations can be agents of reconciliation, who open the doorways to growth for everyone in the fellowship.

Clergy And Laity Differences

There is one other category of differences that congregations need to deal with. There is an all too common tendency to put distance between the laity and the clergy. Laity are sometimes guilty of either pedestalizing (to view as kingly) or trivializing (to view as common) the clergy. Either extreme results in a diminished pastoral effectiveness. It might be helpful for a sensitive lay leader to ask the pastor: When have we done either of these? How might we avoid either pedestalizing or trivializing you?

Of course pastors contribute in some fashion to the way they are perceived by lay persons. Some pastors have strong ego needs to be seen as powerful, in charge, or attractive. Perhaps, because of basic insecurity, some pastors make an issue of their ordination or office as setting them apart (over? above?) from the laity. If the laity participates willingly in this collusion, a situation results in which the pit between the pulpit and the pew is deepened and widened.

I am not interested in diminishing in any way a sense of holy calling and the significance of ordination. I am interested, however, in clergy functioning as members of the human race. My hunch is that whenever a member of the clergy views the laity as threats to his/her ministry and leadership in the congregation, there is, down deep, a basic lack of ego strength or self-confidence.

Pastors often struggle with low self-esteem. Some congregations don't know how to be affirming. The pastor's work is never finished, and it is difficult to guage "success." Beginning pastors, and others to a lesser extent, struggle with questions such as: What am I supposed to be doing? What do the people expect of me? How much influence do I have? Am I liked? Is the church growing?

Whenever a member of the clergy climbs upon a pedestal (or is put there by adoring parishioners) and sends out the message, "follow my leadership, meet my needs, reach my goals," that congregation and pastor are headed for some painful times. Conversely, whenever the laity reduces a pastor to a flunky and sends him/her the message, "serve us, reach our goals, meet our needs," that congregation and pastor are headed for some painful times.

What is needed, then, is a partnership in ministry. Partners are not in a struggle for authority. Partners don't get hung up on roles. Partners don't pedestalize nor trivialize. Partners recognize the uniqueness of the calling to the laity, and the calling to ordination. They value the differences of each. In that setting the congregation will grow in grace, in self-esteem, and likely, in numbers.

IV. Believers need to find ways to minister to each other.

Yes! Lay people *can* minister to each other. Lay people can also minister to clergy. How?

We normally don't think in terms of the laity ministering to the clergy, do we? In order for it to happen, pastors will need to trust lay people for the nurture they need. In most congregations there likely will be several persons who can support, encourage, confront, and guide the pastor, if they are invited to do so. Ray Bullock often told me I was the "second best preacher in the Church of God." He never said who was first, but I always felt affirmed, and I tried harder!

Two or three individuals or a small group of persons might be designated as prayer partners by the pastor. The pastor could meet personally every week or so with the individuals, or meet as a group on a regular basis (perhaps every other week). The participants might need to resist the temptation to use the time for anything other than listening to each other and listening to God.

For a pastor to initiate such prayer support, she/he must have decided that there really is a need for such engagement with the laity, and that the laity are willing and capable of such ministry. Pastor, do you trust your people at this level? Are you convinced that the Spirit can use them to minister to you?

On several occasions I asked persons, like Fern Erickson, to read articles and books for me and then share the contents. I found this very helpful in finding stories, illustrations, and quotations. Ercil Harper was especially good at marking a book and writing notes on the inside of the cover, that assisted me in sermon preparation. When invited to do so, lay people are often very willing to share the best of their own reading with their pastor.

For this sort of ministry to work, there needs to be an openness to it by all parties, plus a degree of vulnerability on the part of the pastor that invites it. It takes the kind of pastor who is human enough or humble enough to reach out for help. The pastor must be willing to say, "I can't do this by myself, will you help me?"

Let me summarize by suggesting that lay persons minister to clergy when they:

1. Pray faithfully for (with) her/him;
2. Support the programs of the congregation with their time, talent, and treasure;
3. Insist that the pastor set aside an hour each day for prayer, relaxation, and visioning;
4. Insist that the pastor set aside a full day every few weeks for prayer, relaxation, and visioning;
5. Insist that once every year, the pastor set aside two or three days for a personal retreat for prayer, relaxation, and visioning; (This is in addition to vacations, conferences, or meetings.)
6. Insist that at seven-year intervals, the pastor be granted a sabbatical leave of three to six months;
7. Not only insist on sabbaticals but support the pastor by prayer, accept the absences, and provide adequate expense allowances;
8. Respect his/her evening hours;
9. Form a pastoral support group for the purpose of listening, sharing, praying, growing;
10. Affirm and confront as appropriate, within a relationship of equals (brothers and sisters in Christ).

Is my dream of "partnership ministry" unrealistic? Can we minister to each other as together we serve? I believe it will work for you. It did for me. I have been ministered to many, many times. When I was young and inexperienced, the lay people were patient. When I was tired and frustrated, they were understanding. When I got sick, they lifted the load. When

I was mistaken or critical, they forgave. When I preached poorly they complimented me. Not always, of course, and not everybody. But the churches I served did more for me than I for them, I think. For that, I'm grateful.

But there are many pastors who struggle in congregations with a limited vision, without adequate resources, and with little hope for change. The load is too heavy, the pay is too skimpy, and the people are unpredictable. Pastor, are you ready for a partnership ministry? You can begin it with one praying lay person. Lay leader, are you ready to go into partnership with your pastor? She/he may be in real need of it today.

V. Believers need to find ways for the expression of feelings.
The fact is, we Christians are fearful of our emotions. We are reluctant to express deep feelings. For one thing, feelings are very personal, and we are not sure that we can trust others to handle them carefully. Also, we have been taught that the expression of feelings is "weak." The truly disciplined person controls emotions, keeps a stiff upper lip. So, we learn to cover up, or pretend. We wear masks and exercise control so that others will not know what is happening deep down inside.

When we gather for worship, many of us are afraid to laugh or cry, rejoice or mourn. Our services too often lack celebration. Thank God for poets, musicians, architects, and artists, who add light and beauty, symbol and sound to our lives and our worship!

Centuries of church history have been written as dates, events, places, and philosophies. Only recently have we begun to value history and theology written and told as story — the story of people, their experiences, their feelings, their fears, their hopes, their relationships. To record *that* something happened is not nearly as valuable as to tell *how* it happened, to *whom*, and what the *response* was. Can we find ways to share our own spiritual stories? Can we be free enough to express ourselves fully to the gathered community? *How* can we learn to share our stories?

It might help if congregations were taught that emotions were intended to be expressed. The Creator never intended that emotions (tenderness, fear, anger, love, joy) be kept inside, in bondage to a misguided intellect. Rather, the intention was that we learn to *express* all the emotions *responsibly*. Many of us learned early that Christians *should not* get angry or have lustful thoughts. But we were not helped with handling those feelings. So we got uptight, guilty, and unhealthy.

It might help if congregations were taught that feelings are neither moral nor immoral — they are amoral. The feelings just *are*. What behaviors we choose as a result of any of the feelings are moral or immoral. Choices may be right or wrong. Feelings are neither.

It might help if congregations were taught the principles of conflict management. It is inevitable that believers will disagree. Our differences practically guarantee that. But if we could learn that conflict is best resolved by talking with each other, rather than distancing from each other, we could grow spiritually. The tendency is, when negative feelings emerge, to walk away — resign from the committee, or change churches. Conflict is precisely the time when we need to be walking *toward* each other, talking and listening and praying. And in the process, we are likely to reveal some feelings. If so, good, for we've gotten honest with each other!

It might help if congregations were taught the ministry of affirmation. Why are so many of us so reluctant to say, ''I appreciate you,'' or ''I love you,'' or, ''Thanks for being the kind of person you are?'' To affirm is to express deep feelings about another person. And that scares us, doesn't it? But the congregation is such a good place to affirm others! *We* need to give it. *Others* need to receive it. Besides, there is much that is positive, beautiful, noble, and helpful about believers. Let's say it to each other! People who have received affirmation can also accept confrontation. Jesus knew the value of affirmation. He called the disciples friends (John 15:14) and brothers (Matthew 23:8).

It might help if congregations were led to worship expressively. What is needed is greater participation. Let the singing, responses, and unison acts of worship be such that everyone will gladly join in. Also, remember that persons can respond and participate silently by internal dialogue, reflecting, praying, reading, and such like.

This is certainly not to suggest that worshippers be invited to respond aloud to every internal prompting or whim. That would be chaotic. Participation can be planned into the structure. I strongly believe that if worship leaders would spend as much time, energy, and expense in getting *all* of the congregation to participate in worship, as they do in getting a *few* people to perform for the rest of us, our worship would be revitalized.

Corporate worship services provide opportunities for congregations to learn how to worship — together or privately. But liturgists, soloists, and preachers need to get out of the way and let the worshippers worship. Too often, they are conscious of their "performance." Too often, congregations are taught to be "spectators." A few minutes of silence during the service might provide persons an opportunity to participate in a worship experience that meets their deepest needs. Leaders might contribute best by being less conspicuous.

VI. Believers need to understand the budgeting realities of spiritual formation.

I was talking recently with the pastor of a medium-sized congregation. He said that he had no hesitation about scheduling a missions convention, or a revival series, or a Christian education conference, because he knew the people would support it with their attendance and offerings. But a spiritual growth conference? He was afraid the crowd would be sparse, and besides, the finance committee probably would not underwrite something unknown like this.

Realistically, spirituality is not likely to generate a lot of excitement and big offerings. Congregations may as well understand that this emphasis may appeal to only a few pilgrims in the group. In fact, praying may never be as popular as preaching. In recent years I've been encouraging congregations and pastors to schedule Quiet Days as a part of their deeper life programming. Participants are instructed in the disciplines of silence, meditation, solitude, and prayer. The group waits quietly to hear God's voice by means of Scripture, other persons, music, readings, and reflection. From the fast lane to a few hours like this may be healing and renewing to weary believers.

Spiritual people in the congregation may be compared to leaven in the bread. What a difference a few praying people can make! There are many very capable pastors who have not been introduced to the notion of programming for spiritual formation. They are not *against* spiritual formation, they are just uninformed. Neither should we expect all denominational leaders to be sensitized to spirituality. Some are, of course, but it is not one of the priority programs, generally. So, as you think of your congregation, be content to start small. After all, great revivals have been known to break out after one person prayed faithfully.

If a few people in the church can see the vision for spiritual formation programming, and budget accordingly, then good things can happen. On the horizon one can see signs of hungering pilgrims seeking after the deeper life, and finding help. A significant movement in spirituality is gaining momentum. As my good friend Loren Rohr says, "Better days are ahead!"

VII. Believers need help with their world view.
We are prone to see the trees but fail to appreciate the forest. We get caught up in the immediate but have no vision for the eternal. Congregations need to be helped with an understanding of spirituality that gets beyond the present moment and the immediate environment. They need a view of spirituality that goes beyond personal needs and preferences. They need to gain an understanding of spirituality that includes the larger world.

It is possible to be seduced by a spirituality of withdrawal or escape. The notion of getting away for prayer and rest entices those who have tired bodies and weary spirits. An ascetic theology which seeks to avoid the world (worldliness) sometimes provides a rationale for ignoring the context of our lives. But there is also the call to serve and change society. So we need a spirituality that will energize us and compel us *into* the world.

David Bosch, summarized Newbigin's (Leslie Newbigin, 1977) contrasting of the "Pilgrim's Progress Model" and the "Jonah Model" of spirituality. Pilgrim, you remember, felt called to escape from the "wicked city." Jonah felt called to enter the city, with all its wickedness and turmoil. Bosch concludes:

> *... the two are absolutely indivisible. The involvement in this world should lead to a deepening of our relationship with and dependence on God, and the deepening of this relationship should lead to increasing involvement in the world (Bosch, 1979, p. 13).*

This apparent paradox may be examined biblically by looking, for example, at what John meant when he said, "avoid the world," but, "meet the world's needs" (1 John 2:15 and 3:17). Also, Jesus instructed his disciples to both "go" (Matthew 28:19) and "tarry" (Acts 1:4). Apparently we are expected to look both ways.

Maybe it is necessary to engage in a sort of rhythm — into the world on mission, then withdraw for awhile for replenishment. Of course, it is not that simplistic. For, in a sense, we are renewed *as we serve*, and we serve when we are only waiting in prayer.

In order for congregations to experience spirituality with a vision, they need to develop a mission consciousness with a global perspective. This consciousness needs to include an awareness of and compassion for all of God's inhabited earth — close at home and far away. A global compassion that neglects the poor, the abused, and the disenfranchised on our doorstep, is unrealistic. Congregations need to be informed, inspired, and mobilized on behalf of righteousness, justice, and opportunity, *wherever* there are human needs.

VIII. Believers need help in managing stress.

I think that bad theology produces much of the stress that Christians experience. Some of the most sincere, dedicated, hard working people I've met know very little about grace. I think it would please God, and we could be more effective as ministers, if we could unload some of our stress.

It might help to *revise* our theology. Have you ever done a comprehensive study of forgiveness, grace and love? Especially as it relates to *you*? I urge you to study these themes, but beyond that, *experience* them. Do you *feel* forgiven and loved? Are you so caught up in "oughts" that you feel guilty much of the time? We *can* live graced lives. We *can* experience peace, now. It is God's gift to us.

It might help to *reorder* our priorities. Often, our stress level is in direct proportion to the number of our wants. The secret is to want less! We really could get by with fewer things. The world will go on even though we do not get our way. If only we could want more of God, and less of everything else, our stress level would go down.

It might help to *resist* the cultural trends. Our world (and sometimes the church) sends us a powerful message: Possess, manage, be successful. It is generally better to go against the stream of what "everybody" is doing. For the church to be salt and light, we must resist being swallowed up in the world's pressure to conform (Romans 12:2).

The Christian virtue of gentleness is a good antidote to stressful living. Gentleness may not be very popular, but it is powerful. Adrian van Kaam provides a beautiful description of this virtue which is so essential to spiritual development.

Gentleness does not occur on the periphery of my life but at its core, where God is present to me. It is not an ornament, a frivolous extra for nicety's sake, but an essential part of human life as called forth by the Divine Gentleness.

Lord, let me find back
The lost treasure of time:
Time for gentle listening to a friend,
For sharing the play of a child,
For consoling a suffering fellow man,
For thinking without strain,
For labor without pressure.
Time to delight in birds and flowers,
Blooming trees and lustrous green.
Time to enjoy music, friends, and meals,
Time to be silent and alone,
Time to be quietly at home,
Time to be present to your mystery.
Free me from the tyranny
Of time urgency.
Let time not possess me,
Neither the pressure of daily concerns.
Let me not cram every moment
With useful or exciting things
To do or say.
Let my life be a gentle preparation
For the pure and precious moments
Of listening to you,
So that I may not drown
In the rushing waters
Of practical pursuits.
(Adrian van Kaam, 1974, p. 36-37).

Conclusion

In this chapter I have said that congregations can nurture the spiritual growth of its members. I have made some suggestions that might help persons minister to each other, and, thus, facilitate spiritual wholeness. The pastor is the key person in all this. The congregation will likely not move beyond the pastor in spiritual vitality. He/she is the key spiritual educator, model, and director. May every congregation be so fortunate as to have a pastor who is on a pilgrimage to the heart of God. Spiritual formation takes place best in a safe, sanctified community.

Conclusion

Writing a book has been an intimidating, laborious, rewarding adventure. It has been an exercise in self-disclosure and risk. I have written with passion. I care deeply for ministers. I really do appreciate the fact that there are thousands of servant-leaders out there giving their lives to the church and to the whole of God's creation. It matters to me that you are there, and that we've connected in this way. I pray that this book has brought a little light and warmth along your journey.

With the Apostle Paul, my prayer for you is that, "He who has begun a good work in you will complete it ... and that your love may abound still more and more in knowledge and all discernment ..." (see Philippians 1:3-11).

Let us admit that many of the traditional practices of spirituality were forged at the anvil of medieval experience. The world view that medieval mystics possessed is not the same that is prevalent today. In these days when a sophisticated rationalistic-materialistic-humanistic perspective on faith is widespread in the church, how can we invite persons to the old beliefs and practices?

To discount the old on the basis of age alone makes no sense. Neither does grasping the new for newness alone. However, each culture and each generation needs to reframe traditional theology, and recast traditional methods, in order to meet the needs of contemporary believers. Traditions are steps on the way, and thus must be left behind as it were, when new steps are sought and discovered. But being traditional people, we carry the influences of the past with us, even as we create new methods of piety. We look back not so much as collectors of antiques but as architects seeking for new ideas. But in the meantime, the "old paths" (Jeremiah 6:16) provide us with security, inspiration, and guidance.

What is needed, then, is a spirituality for the freeway. Maybe pilgrim metaphors do not communicate to a technological society. But even freeways have entrance and exit ramps, rest areas, regulatory signs, and weary travelers. We still have the disciplines with us, and they work whether we're on a path or a freeway. There is little empirical evidence on which to guarantee positive results from practicing the disciplines. And that is precisely why we speak of "walking by faith." So, while there is no guarantee of results, there is a promise of a relationship (Matthew 28:20), and a series of experiences.

I am often reminded of Dietrich Bonhoeffer's pregnant statement: "all historical events are penultimate." If that is true, then all events, all behaviors, all church programs, all seminary curricula, all ministerial efforts and such like, have an ultimate significance that is beyond the present intersection of time, space, and event. Thus, reality always has a quality of "beyondness," and Christian leaders are always in search of a reality that is beyond the now.

Jesus spoke of this beyondness, when he said,

> *You search the Scriptures . . . but you are not willing to come to me (John 5:39-40).*

I'm sure Jesus did not intend, by this statement, to minimize scholarship, nor human effort to understand religious knowledge. But I think he was suggesting that intellectual pursuit might be likened to a series of doors through which we pass on our way to meet the Master. Knowing about is not the goal. Meeting is!

I sincerely hope that my writing has been clear and meaningful. I am aware that I am a crusader on behalf of the experiential (affective, relational, mystical) aspects of the Christian life. I trust that my rather consistent inclination toward the intuitive-feeling approach hasn't been a problem for you.

Parker Palmer, in a chapter on "The Spiritual Formation of Teachers," has this to say:

> *But the original and authentic meaning of the word 'professor' is, 'one who professes a faith.' The true professor is not one who controls facts and theories and techniques. The true professor is one who affirms a transcendent center of truth, a center that lies beyond our contriving, that enters history through the lives of those who profess it and brings us into community with each other and the world. If professors are to create a space in which obedience to truth is practiced, we must become 'professors' again. To do so, we must cultivate personal experience of that which we need to profess (Palmer, 1983, p. 113).*

And what we leaders need to "profess" is that there is life in Christ! In order to "profess" it, we first need to experience it. Which leads me to ask again: What is the integrating center of your ministry? What pulls it all together? For some persons it may be preaching, or intellectual pursuits. For others it may be creative expression, theological dialogue, interpersonal relationships, or social activism. I suggest that the spiritual formation of the minister is the best option for an integrating center. The bottom line, then, is our life in Christ!

Let me summarize some recurring themes I have tried to address, sometimes indirectly, that I trust have come through to you as affirmations.

1. The notion of friendship with God is at the heart of spiritual formation. Not all Christians in all ages have understood nor related to God in friendly ways. I have tried to sketch spirituality in less legalistic, less ritualistic terms. I really do believe that the concept of spiritual friendship catches up much of what I've been trying to say about our relationship with God.

2. We are created to function in a God-ordained rhythm — labor and rest, involvement and detachment, community

and solitude. We live fulfilled, effective, happy lives, only as we function in a balanced, rhythmic fashion.

3. There is a basic need to know God. This universal religious impulse or drive has been expressed in many different ways, but I like the way Blaise Pascal put it: There is a God-shaped emptiness in all of humankind which only God can fill. We are continuously being drawn to God, even as we are constantly searching for satisfying relationship with God.

4. Depending upon our personalities and cultural conditioning (and perhaps other factors), we tend to vacillate between an active (kataphatic) and a receptive (apophatic) approach to God. Should we be initiators or receivers? Both of course, and the goal is balance.

5. Our society presents many polarities, ambiguities, and fragmentations. With the dissonance in our lives, there is often disharmony in our souls. But the gospel message is one of wholeness. *Hindsight* is valuable; *foresight* is needed; but *wholesight* is essential! Wholesight is spirit-enabled, the result of praying. Prayer helps us put all of life together.

6. The Bible is a major source for our formation and we need to become at home in it (John 8:31). While Jesus' meaning here is apparently not limited to the Bible, I think it surely includes it. His message is: "If you are at home in my word, then you are my disciples."

7. The long view is superior to the short view. How earthbound and time-bound is our vision! We need to listen to what the ages have to tell us, and to what scripture promises. A healthy spirituality is acquainted with the saints of the past and is open to what God is currently doing.

8. In ministry, ultimately, loving may be enough. (I recommend a devotional reading of the Johannine writings at this point.) In the final analysis, our ultimate need is to be loved, and our ultimate accomplishment is to give love. Spiritual formation is cultivating this loving relationship with God, God's world, and God's people. Ministry is giving back that love in service to God, God's world, and God's people. I don't know how to make it simpler, nor more profound!

9. Prayer helps to integrate life, ministry, and faith.

Why do I promote prayer when ministers are already so terribly busy? Why do I think spiritual formation is so essential? The fact is, we are busy — too busy — and we *are* being formed. But formed by what? By whom? How? How much are we being shaped by our temporary culture rather than by the eternal? While we are looking forward to heaven, we're participating in eternity now. At least, that is our desire. "Eternal life is this: to know you, the only true God, and him whom you have sent, Jesus Christ" (John 17:3).

The whole devotional enterprise has been faulted for allegedly fostering personal piety and an individualism that strikes at the foundations of community, congregation, and accountability. But the need for connectedness, for mutual encouragement, and for spiritual friendships (which I have discussed in this book) is precisely that aspect of spirituality (often neglected) which will be useful in combatting the irresponsible individualism that is so common in the contemporary church.

I am not attempting to lead you along a path of feel-good Christianity nor emotionalism. There is more to faith than feelings. But I would like to support those who believe that the experiential approach to reality is a valid one. I'd like to support those who have had an experience of the strangely warmed heart, but are having difficulty finding an adequate vocabulary to analyze or describe it. I'd like to encourage those who *know intuitively* that they know God, but get frustrated with the interminable, technical, and often confusing conversations about the transcendence, omnipotence, and immutability of God.

God is alive and at work. I frequently encounter persons who are living abundant lives in Christ. They are not victims of theological illusions nor psychological delusions. They are real people with an authentic faith. Listen. You, too, may hear the sound of angels. You may be overtaken with a profound mystery. You may experience a miracle. Listen, for God is within you. God is not "out there" somewhere. Your discovery that God is near may be the beginning of life as it was meant to be lived.

Epilogue

"God does not ask anything of you except that you let yourself go and let God be God in you" (Meister Eckhart).

APPENDICES

Appendix A

Evaluation And Feedback

One of the first tasks of the minister is to "know thyself." We grow in self-awareness by regularly engaging in introspective experiences. Self-evaluation, examination of conscience, meditation, journaling, solicitation of feedback and spiritual direction will contribute to knowing oneself.

This Appendix contains some suggestions for persons asking "What kind of person am I," and "Am I the kind of person who can be effective as a minister?" Are you ready to seek feedback and evaluation as a means of spiritual growth?

Evaluation is at the heart of personal, spiritual and professional growth. Some people object to being critiqued and get defensive when suggestions are made. That is a sure sign of immaturity! Sometimes it *is* painful to be evaluated. But it is essential to development.

I recommend that beginning ministers seek evaluation of their interpersonal skills, leadership style, preaching, dress and appearance, and so on. Better to seek it, than for someone to give it unsolicited!

We really can learn from each other, and we really do need to listen to each other. Notice that evaluation contains "value." One mark of a growing Christian is the ability to ask for, receive, and use responsible critique.

Survey: Expectations Of The Pastor's Role

How important is each pastoral function to you? Circle 5 if you think it is extremely important; 1 if you think it is unimportant; 2, 3, or 4 if your estimate is in between.

1. Teaches and works directly with adults in   1 2 3 4 5
   adult religious education classes and/or
   special seminar series.

2. Participates in community projects and or- 1 2 3 4 5
   ganizations (such as school boards, community involvement).

3. Ministers to the sick, dying, and bereaved. 1 2 3 4 5

4. Leads public worship.   1 2 3 4 5

5. Works with congregational boards and   1 2 3 4 5
   committees.

6. Maintains a disciplined program of prayer   1 2 3 4 5
   and personal devotion.

7. Accepts speaking engagements before com- 1 2 3 4 5
   munity and civic groups, for special community occasions or for radio and television.

8. Oversees church office activities, church   1 2 3 4 5
   bulletins, correspondence, records, etc.

9. Tries to maintain harmony and resolve   1 2 3 4 5
   conflict among church members over
   church programs, finances, elections, etc.

10. Preaches sermons.   1 2 3 4 5

11. Visits new residents and recruits new   1 2 3 4 5
    members.

12. Counsels with people about their personal   1 2 3 4 5
    problems.

13. Follows a disciplined program of continu- 1 2 3 4 5
    ing education.

14. Teaches and works directly with children,   1 2 3 4 5
    visits Sunday School, preaches children's
    sermons, etc.

15. Assists victims of social neglect, injustice,   1 2 3 4 5
    and prejudice; cooperates with social ser-
    vice and charitable programs.

16. Teaches and works directly with young   1 2 3 4 5
    people (junior high and high school age) in
    classes and/or fellowship groups.

17. Administers baptism and communion, con-   1 2 3 4 5
    ducts weddings and funerals.

18. Cultivates a home and personal life includ-   1 2 3 4 5
    ing friends and interests outside church ac-
    tivities.

19. Leads financial drives and building   1 2 3 4 5
    programs.

20. Talks with individuals about their spiritual   1 2 3 4 5
    development, religious life and beliefs.

21. Participates in denominational activities   1 2 3 4 5
    and conferences.

22. Presents denominational programs to con-   1 2 3 4 5
    gregation.

23. Helps plan church budget and manage   1 2 3 4 5
    church finances.

24. Fosters fellowship at church gatherings.   1 2 3 4 5

25. Serves as an example of high moral and   1 2 3 4 5
    ethical character.

26. Maps out objectives and plans overall   1 2 3 4 5
    church strategy and program.

27. Interests capable people in church activi-   1 2 3 4 5
    ties; recruits, trains, and assists lay leaders.

28. Visits regularly in the homes of the congre-   1 2 3 4 5
    gation.

29. Counsels people facing major decisions of   1 2 3 4 5
life, such as marriage and vocation.

30. Supplies new ideas for activities and   1 2 3 4 5
projects.

31. Promotes enthusiasm for church activities. 1 2 3 4 5

Now that you have completed this survey, go back and put a big check on the left side of the page before each of the 5 statements most important to you. Discuss your responses with a friend or mentor.

Feedback

"Feedback" is a way of helping another person to consider changing his/her behavior. It is communication to a person which gives that person information about how he/she affects others. Feedback helps an individual keep behavior "on target," and thus better achieve goals. It may be written, or given verbally. To do both, is to increase accuracy in communication and to increase effectiveness.

Some criteria for useful feedback:

1. It is descriptive rather than evaluative. By reporting one's own reaction, it leaves the individual free to use it or not use it as he/she sees fit. By avoiding evaluative language, it reduces the need for the individual to react defensively.

2. It is specific rather than general. To be told that one is "dominating" will probably not be as useful as to be told that "just now when we were deciding the issue you did not listen to what others said and I felt forced to accept your arguments or face attack from you."

3. It takes into account the needs of both the receiver and giver of feedback. Feedback can be destructive when it serves only our own needs and fails to consider the needs of the person on the receiving end.

4. It is directed toward behavior which the receiver can do something about. Frustration is only increased when a person is reminded of some shortcoming over which he/she has no control.

5. It is solicited, rather than imposed. Feedback is most useful when the receiver has formulated the kind of question which those observing can answer.

6. It is well timed. In general, feedback is most useful at the earliest opportunity after the given behavior (depending, of course, on the person's readiness to hear it, support available from others, etc.)

7. It is checked to insure clear communication. One way of doing this is to have the receiver try to rephrase the feedback that has been received to see if it corresponds to what the sender had in mind.

8. When feedback is given in a group, both giver and receiver have opportunity to check with others in the group the accuracy of the feedback. Is this one person's impression, or an impression shared by others?

9. It is assumed that feedback can be given to persons not known well by the giver. In that instance, it is feedback based on initial impressions. It is nonetheless valid, and valuable, especially for those whose vocations involve meeting new people.

Feedback, then, is a way of giving help; it is a corrective mechanism for the individual who wants to learn how well behavior matches intentions; and it is a means of understanding how one is perceived by others.

Feedback For Growth

To: ________________________ Date: ________________________

(Please give me feedback by answering these questions as honestly and completely as you can. I will do my best to accept it gracefully and objectively. Thanks for helping me know more about myself!)

1. How do you see me as a person? How do I come across? Describe typical behaviors.

2. What do you experience when you're around me? How do you feel in my presence? Describe typical attitudes.

3. Give me some suggestions that I might consider, such as:

   I'd like to see you try ...:

   I could relate to you better if ...:

   You could be a warmer, friendlier person if ...:

   You would come across more "professional" if ...:

   You would come across more "ministerial" if ...:

4. Any other information you'd like to share? Questions you'd like to ask of me?

From: ________________________

A Theology Of Ministry

The formulation of a theology of ministry is both an entering concern for the beginning minister as well as a continuing concern for the experienced one. It is essential to ask: What am I called to do and why? How do I begin?

The leader continually needs to be asking the following questions. The answers do not come easily nor finally. What follows are some guidelines and sources for the person seeking to initiate or clarify a Theology of Ministry.

A Theology of Ministry needs to be shaped by at least the following influences:

1. **Scripture.** What are the biblical principles, mandates, and guidelines that are shaping your ministerial formation?

2. **Experience.** What are the turning points in your formation history that influence who you are and how you do ministry? Who are the significant others, and what are the crucial experiences?

3. **Tradition.** What have you learned from and in what sense are you a product of the universal stream of wisdom? What about your particular faith-roots?

4. **Reason.** How do the various sciences inform your practice of ministry? What do critical thinking and technology have to do with the practice of ministry?

5. **Context.** How does your cultural environment shape your practice of ministry?

6. **Discernment.** How are you led by the Spirit to interpret, integrate, and implement your theology of ministry?

Based on these and other influences, the minister responds with certain actions, which continue to shape his/her theology. Theology cannot be formed well in the abstract. Rather, it develops in the crucible of life. What follows are some of the things one needs to *do* in order to create a holistic theology of ministry.

1. Submit to the authority of God and God's Word. Full obedience to the God of Scripture is essential to personal and professional formation for ministry.

2. Respond to a Divine Call. The nature of this call is unique for each person, but it is essential to have sensed a summons from God.

3. Inquire into the nature of the church. Since it is intended that ministry be practiced in and through the church, it is necessary to understand what it is (the reconciled), what it does (reconciliation), and how it works (theocratically, charismatically).

4. Examine the nature and function of vocation. What are the long-term implications of being called to ministry?

5. Engage in continuing preparation. What is the basic academic, skill, and character formation necessary for entrance into and continuation in ministry?

6. Develop trust. Be in the process of building trust in God, trust of others, and trust in self, along with leading others to do the same.

7. Be intentional in the disciplines of the deeper life.

For further reading:

Oden, Thomas C.

1983 *Pastoral Theology*. Harper and Row.

Oglesby, Wm. B.

1969 *The New Shape of Pastoral Theology*. Abingdon.

Shelp, Earl and Ronald Sunderland.

1981 *A Biblical Basis for Ministry*. Westminster.

Tidball, Derek. J.

1986 *Skillful Shepherds*. Zondervan.

Appendix C
An Accountability Covenant

To My Spiritual Friend:

I am placing this sheet in your hands in order to indicate what I really want and need from you as my spiritual director. I have given this my serious thought and prayer. I am seeking to make my spiritual formation intentional, rather than incidental. I am trusting you to become the instrument of God to assist my pilgrimage "in Christ." I am mindful, however, that it is the Holy Spirit upon whom we both rely as the supreme director of our souls.

Each time we meet, please find ways to inquire of me concerning one or more of the following areas of my life. You have my permission to confront me and to offer feedback. Your suggestions and prayers are valued.

I. Inner Disciplines

    A. Meditation
    B. Prayer
    C. Fasting
    D. Study

II. Outer Disciplines

    A. Simple Lifestyle
    B. Solitude
    C. Submission
    D. Service

III. Corporate Disciplines

    A. Confession
    B. Worship
    C. Celebration
    D. Guidance

IV. Character Disciplines

    A. Love
    B. Joy
    C. Peace
    D. Patience
    E. Kindness
    F. Goodness
    G. Faithfulness
    H. Gentleness
    I. Self-Control

V. Ministerial Disciplines

    A. Witnessing
    B. Caring
    C. Visioning
    D. Leading
    E. Equipping

Signature: ___________________________________

Date: ___________________________________

Director's Name: ___________________________________

Meetings: ___________________________________

____

Anderson School of Theology   Dwight L. Grubbs
Spiritual Friends Program   Dir. of Spiritual Life

Appendix D

Type And Ministry

I have found a study of Jung's work on typology, and the use of materials based on his theories, to be helpful for ministers. The Myers-Briggs Type Inventory (MBTI) is a most useful instrument. I recommend it for several reasons.

First, it helps us recognize and value human differences. The differences among us can be viewed as strengths. We can appreciate the fact that God gifts each of us uniquely. The appreciation of these differences help us to build strong relationships with others in spite of these differences.

Second, an understanding of our own personality type enables us to understand how we think and decide and to work on our own weaknesses. It also helps us identify our strengths, and design spiritual growth plans suitable to ourselves.

Third, as leaders, we become better spiritual guides when we understand how others think, and pray, and decide.

For an introduction to the MBTI and personality types, I suggest the books by Kiersey and Bates, Michael and Norrisey, Robert and Carol Faucett and Myers listed in the Bibliography.

Information about the MBTI and materials for using it might be obtained from:

> Consulting Psychologists Press
> 577 College Ave.
> Palo Alto, CA 94306-1490

> Center for Application of Psychological Types
> Box 13807 University Station
> Gainesville, FL 32604

> Christian Laity of Chicago
> Dr. Hal Edwards
> 1437 West 37th St.
> Chicago, IL 60609

A Guide To Discovering And Using Spiritual Gifts

I.   A Perspective on Gifts Theology

The biblical doctrine of the Holy Spirit's gifts needs to be clearly articulated in the church. Functionally speaking, however, the Spirit operates in the realm of experience in gifting believers. Doctrines may be easier to clarify than experiences. So, gifts theology may be confusing, even divisive, for those who demand theological precision. If, however, we can accept the multiformity of spiritual gifts and the diversity of their expression within the church, then an amazing vitality will emerge. It needs to be kept in mind that spiritual gifts are for the Body, not so much for the individual. (Much of the following material is adapted from C. Peter Wagner.)

II.   Do I have a gift or gifts?

>   1 Corinthians 12:1; 4-7
>   Ephesians 4:7-8
>   1 Peter 4:10-11

III. Definition.

A spiritual gift is an ability (grace) divinely bestowed upon a believer in order that the Body (church) may be enabled to fulfill its mission.

IV.   What are the gifts?

>   A. General Support Gifts (Ephesians 4:11-16)
>   1. Apostles
>   2. Prophets
>   3. Evangelists
>   4. Pastor-Teachers

B. Sign Gifts (1 Corinthians 12:8-10)
  5. Miracles
  6. Healings
  7. Tongues
  8. Interpretation of Tongues

C. Service or Working Gifts (1 Corinthians 12:1-10;
   28; Romans 12:6-8)
  9. Wisdom — the ability to gain insight as to
     how to use knowledge in the Body.
  10. Knowledge — the ability to discover, ac-
      cumulate and clarify information.
  11. Faith — the ability to see the possibilities in
      the will and purposes of God.
  12. Prophecy — the ability to receive and com-
      municate God's message to God's people.
  13. Discernment — the ability to understand hu-
      man personality and how the Spirit is at
      work in persons.
  14. Helps — the ability to invest one's life in
      the lives of others.
  15. Teaching — the ability to communicate in-
      formation and experience.
  16. Administration — the ability to lead in set-
      ting goals and accomplishing them.
  17. Giving — the ability to give of themselves
      and their material resources.
  18. Exhortation — the ability to comfort, en-
      courage, counsel.
  19. Leadership — the ability to get people to
      work together and achieve.
  20. Mercy — the ability to feel empathy and to
      translate compassion into deeds.
  21. Service — the ability to identify unmet
      needs of persons and to mobilize
      resources.
  22. Celibacy — the ability to remain single and
      fulfilled.

23. Voluntary poverty — the ability to renounce material comforts and live on the poverty level of their society.
24. Intercession — the ability to pray for others regularly and over an extended period of time.
25. Hospitality — the ability to provide a safe space and a warm welcome.
26. Martyrdom — the ability to undergo suffering, even death, for the faith.
27. Exorcism — the ability to cast out evil spirits.
28. Missionary — the ability to minister in a second culture.

V.   How can I discover my gift(s)?

While gifts are bestowed by the grace of God, it is the recipient's responsibility to identify the gifts and present oneself for further equipping. The following "steps" might be helpful in this process of accepting, understanding, and employing the Holy Spirit's gifts.

A. Conversion. Gifts are for believers only, those who have repented of all sin, received forgiveness, and begun the new life in Christ.

B. Commitment. An attitude of willingness to be used of God is a pre-requisite to the reception of gifts. The Spirit gifts those who are usable.

C. Prayer and Reflection. There needs to be a process of serious self-examination. What is my sense of vocation? What are my abilities and needs?

D. Study. A careful study of the Scriptures, books on spiritual gifts, and persons in whom the gifts are operative, will provide a sound theological understanding for making decisions.

E. Feedback. What did I learn from the gifts questionnaire? What are other trusted persons saying to me about my gift(s)?

F. Experimentation. Try. Dare to fail. Get help and try again. Secure an evaluation of your effectiveness.

G. Sensitivity. A gift presumes a relationship, so stay in touch with the Holy Spirit. Be conscious of the needs of the Body. Try to be aware of how your gift is being accepted by others.

VI. What is the purpose of the gifts?

In contemporary language, we might say that spiritual gifts provide a workable strategy for church management. When the gifts function as God intended, friction will be minimized, discouragement will decline, and burnout will be reduced. In more biblical language, we might say that, spiritual gifts are for:

A. The equipping of believers (Ephesians 4:11-12).
B. The establishment of believers (Romans 1:11).
C. The edification of the whole congregation (Ephesians 4:12; 16).
D. The encouragement of the leaders (Romans 1:12).
E. The enlargement of the fellowship (Ephesians 4:16).
F. The exaltation of Jesus Christ (1 Peter 4:11).

VII. Some topics for further discussion.

A. What kind of person is a most likely recipient of and effective "user" of spiritual gifts?
B. How might a congregation be functioning when it practices gifts theology?
C. How would you go about introducing a theology of gifts in a local congregation?
D. How would you go about implementing gifts theology into the structure and programming of a congregation?
E. Many persons fear the abuse of gifts. Discuss this reluctance and offer some suggestions for dealing with it.

VIII. Some resources for further study.

Bryant, Charles V.
    1986 *Rediscovering the Charismata.* Word Books.
Hurn, Raymond W.
    1979 *Finding Your Ministry: A Study of the Fruit and Gifts of the Spirit.* Beacon Hill Press.
Kinghorn, Kenneth.
    1975 *Fresh Wind of the Spirit.* Abingdon Press.
    1976 *Gifts of the Spirit.* Abingdon Press.
Steadman, Ray
    1972 *Body Life.* G. L. Publications.
Wagner, C. Peter
    1979 *Your Spiritual Gifts Can Help Your Church Grow.* Regal Books.

Resources For Ministers

Alban Institute
4125 Nebraska Ave. NW
Washington D.C. 20016
1-800-457-8893

Leadership
465 Gunderson Dr.
Carol Stream, IL 60188

The Upper Room
1908 Grand Avenue, Box 189
Nashville, TN 37202

Forward Movement Publications
412 Sycamore St.
Cincinnati, OH 45202

"Weavings"
(A Journal of the Christian Spiritual Life)
PO Box 189
Nashville, TN 37202-0189

Spiritual Formation Resource Packet
Division of Ordained Ministry
PO Box 871
Nashville, TN 37202

Fuller Institute of Evangelism and Church Growth
PO Box 91990
Pasadena, CA 91109

Kirkridge Retreat Center
Bangor, PA 18013
The Shalem Institute for Spiritual Formation
Dr. Tilden W. Edwards, Director
Mount St. Alban
Washington, D.C. 20016

Retreats International
Room 1112, Memorial Library
Notre Dame, IN 46556
  (write for a Directory of Retreat Centers in the United
    States.)

Center for Application of Psychological Type
PO Box 13807, University Station
Gainesville, FL 32601

Consulting Psychologists Press
PO Box 60070
Palo Alto, CA 94306

Midwest Career Development
2501 North Star Rd., Suite 200
Columbus, OH 43221

Center for Parish Development
Dr. Paul Dietterich
5407 So. University Avenue
Chicago, IL 60615

Minister's Life
PO Box 910
Minneapolis, MN 55440

Covenant Discipleship Groups
The General Board of Discipleship
PO Box 840
Nashville, TN 37202

The Epiphany Association
1145 Beechwood Blvd.
Pittsburgh, PA 15206-4517

Appendix G
A Ministerial Self-Analysis

Instructions: Write a substantial paragraph in response to each of the following questions. Respond from the "gut level." Seek to express your deepest feelings, not what you think is expected, or what you ought to say. Resist the temptation to engage in facade-building! Get in touch with your real self. Happy questing!

1. Do you really care for people? Do you like to be around people or do you generally prefer to be alone?

2. Do you view people generally as threats (to be guarded against, watched, critics of you) or as comrades (supporters, encouragers, fellow-ministers)?

3. What are your personal limitations that will affect your ministry?

4. What are your personal strengths that will affect your ministry?

5. Is the world generally good and friendly, or bleak and abrasive?

6. Does the Bible open up the world and life for you or does it define boundaries (restrict life)? Why? How? Elaborate.

7. Do you feel accepted and loved by others, generally? Do you tend to feel forgiven or guilty?

8. Do you feel good (comfortable) when you compliment others and get praise from others? Is it natural for you to express affection (verbally, touching, hugging)?

9. Are you often indecisive, tense, angry for no apparent reason, and seem unable to concentrate on a task?

10. Do you often feel pressured to meet other persons' expectations of you, and are unable to experience freedom to be your own person and to perform your ministry in ways that are fulfilling?

11. What do you do with your angry feelings (frustration, resentment, disappointments) in the context of your ministry?

12. If the expectation is that ministers are supposed to be "good" (loving, spiritual), what do you do with that side of you which is "bad" (the flesh, temptation, shadow side)?

13. Which is more important to you, to be known as a faithful and effective minister, or to be known as a whole, happy, and fulfilled person? Why?

14. How do you determine when you are speaking for God (prophetic) and when you are making reference to God and the Bible as a means of supporting your own perspectives on an issue?

15. Many ministers grow up as socially awkward, who relate to others in a detached way, and who then enter a profession of giving or helping so that other persons will accept them for what they *do*, rather than for who they *are* as persons. How does this relate to you?

Minister's Self-Rating Scale

Rate yourself: 1 (low) to 10 (high)

1. _____ I am often generous with sincere praise for work well done.
2. _____ I sense my own leadership and people generally respond positively.
3. _____ I am usually well-groomed, neat, and appropriately dressed.
4. _____ I usually face up to problems and deal with them, rather than putting off decisions and action.
5. _____ I am usually comfortable and relaxed when I am chairing a business meeting.
6. _____ I can usually find whatever I'm looking for in my study.
7. _____ I have records of how many times I called in the homes of all of my people last year.
8. _____ I set, announce, and keep regular office hours.
9. _____ I have regularly scheduled family times.
10. _____ I begin most of our services, meetings, etc. on time.
11. _____ I usually feel well prepared when I stand to preach.
12. _____ I seldom have to make excuses for not being able to finish a task on time, or not being where I'm supposed to be.
13. _____ I feel comfortable around professionals, persons in authority, and other ministers.
14. _____ I have the ability to laugh at myself.
15. _____ I have the courage to say "no."
16. _____ I usually fall asleep easily and sleep well.
17. _____ I read books and periodicals in order to keep abreast.
18. _____ I maintain confidentiality.
19. _____ I have a lot of good ideas and feel free to suggest them.
20. _____ I have goals set for myself and for our church.

A Voluntary Accountability Covenant

This Covenant is intended to be used by a representative group within a congregation, and its pastor. The creation of this Covenant should be bathed in prayer, and, likely will involve several meetings in order to clarify and express the opinions and hopes of all parties.

The Pastor-Parish Relations Committee or the Church Council will probably represent the congregation in the formulation of this Covenant.

The purpose of the Covenant is to make intentional and formal the desire of the undersigned, to engage in the mutual care of their souls, and the souls of the rest of the congregation.

I. Congregation.

1. In what sense are we individually and corporately accountable to each other and to our pastor in spiritual matters?

2. How is our sense of accountability expressed? For example, do we individually, and as a congregation, maintain intentional programs of spiritual formation? Are we accountable to a spiritual friend or to a small group?

3. Is it our intention to assume the responsibility to nurture, support, encourage, and pray for each other and our pastor(s)?

4. Do we have a group of persons within the congregation (e.g. Spiritual Life Committee, Advisory Council, Elders, Pastor-Parish Relations Committee) designated to carry out the specifics and the spirit of this Accountability Covenant?

II. Pastor.

1. In what sense am I accountable to the congregation in spiritual matters? Do I enter into a partnership with them

for my own spiritual health? Do I invite their evaluations and recommendations?

2. Do I have a mentor, spiritual friend, or support group who watches over my soul and calls me to account for my life in Christ?

3. Do I maintain an intentional program of spiritual formation for myself? What spiritual disciplines am I currently engaged in?

4. Have I made commitments to and established relationships with community, area, state, and national ministerial bodies in order to maintain professional connections with peers, especially at the level of spiritual growth? Have these commitments been written and shared with the appropriate persons?

5. Do I assume the responsibility of becoming spiritual director to the congregation? Practically speaking, how will I do this work?

III. Affirmation.

We have read the above questions and reflected upon them carefully. In a spirit of openness and searching, we have discussed the meanings of this Covenant. Attached is a summary of our written responses to this process. We, the undersigned pastor(s) and laypersons now sign this document, indicating our commitment to support and abide by its intentions.

_________________________________   _________________________________

_________________________________   _________________________________

_________________________________   _________________________________

_________________________________   _________________________________

____

date   location

Appendix J

My Code Of Ethics

As a minister of the Gospel, I pledge my allegiance to Jesus Christ and to God, whose wisdom I seek and whose Spirit I shall invoke on all my relationships. God being my helper, I will seek to abide by the following code of professional pastoral practice.

A. In my personal conduct:
  1. I will maintain a vital spiritual relationship with God by discipline in daily devotions, by prayer, by meditation, and by reading the Scriptures.

  2. I will be honest and fair with all. I will strive in my family relationships to always be a devoted spouse and parent, giving my family the time and consideration to which they are entitled.

  3. I will be Christian in all conduct toward others regardless of race, class, and creed.

  4. I will attempt to be modest in success and gracious in failure.

  5. I will attempt to be a good steward of time, treasure, and talent.

  6. I will endeavor to live within my income and not leave unpaid debts.

  7. I will guard my physical health and personal appearance.

  8. I will strive to grow intellectually by studying, reading, attending conferences, listening, and reflecting with others.

B. In my relationship to the church I serve:
  1. I will remember I am their spiritual leader and not a dictator.

2. I will keep before the church a challenging program of devotion, study, service, and giving.

3. I will preach the Word, be true to my convictions, and exercise compassion for all persons.

4. I will pastor the whole church with favoritism toward none.

5. I will defend the good name of the congregation.

6. I will keep confidences sacred.

C. In my relationship to my fellow ministers:

1. I will cultivate friendships with fellow ministers and work cooperatively with them.

2. I will seek to uphold the dignity of the Christian ministry.

3. I will not gossip about fellow ministers or speak disparagingly about my predecessor or successor.

4. I will give my successor every advantage possible.

5. I will avoid unnecessary and inappropriate visits to my former pastorate.

6. I will not enter into unfair competition with my fellow ministers to secure a pastorate, nor to gain recognition.

7. I will respect the pastoral relationships of my fellow ministers when I visit in their parishes.

D. In my relationship to the community I serve:

1. I will lend my influence and support to community agencies and activities which promote the mutual well being and health of my community.

2. I will speak for right in moral issues and will work for human equality and justice for all.

3. I will fulfill my obligations as a good citizen.

4. I will respect the responsibilities imposed through school, home, and work upon persons living in my parish.

E. In my relationship with my faith group:

1. I will uphold the national program of the Church of God as projected by the General Assembly, keeping myself informed regarding these causes and striving to support them through the resources of the local church.

2. I will seek to foster close relationships with state and district fellowships and judicatories.

F. In my relationship to the church universal:

1. I will reach my hands in fellowship and concern to members of the Universal Church regardless of race, color, national origin or denominational affiliation.

2. I will endeavor to maintain cooperative fellowship with those ecumenical organizations whose purposes are to promote the unity and growth of the body of Christ.

3. I will, as representative of all believers, reach out to the poor, the powerless, the abused, whoever they are, and wherever they may be.

Adapted by: Dwight L. Grubbs, in 1966 at
Anderson School of Theology

Job Description And Working Agreement

I. Introductory Statements

A. This instrument is prepared from the viewpoint that pastoral ministry is a profession. This is not to detract from the Ministry as a calling, but to point out for observation and discussion some facets of the ministerial relationship which are often not understood nor openly discussed.

B. It is assumed that the Pastor is first of all a servant of and a spokesperson for God. Authority is a consequence of a Divine call, faithfulness to God's word, and a life lived in Christ.

C. This is no attempt to put shackles nor controls on God's minister, but rather is an attempt to free him/her from misunderstandings, to prevent the dissemination of misinformation, and to lay the groundwork for an open and continuing dialogue between the minister and the people regarding their mutual ministries.

D. This instrument shall serve as the basis for conversation between the Church Council of the congregation and prospective ministers, as well as the guiding document in subsequent efforts of the Council to maintain wholesome relationships between Pastor and congregation.

II. Pastor-Church Relationships

1. The Pastor will view his/her relationship with the congregation as a ministry with people. The minister shall neither be pedestalized nor trivialized.

2. He/she will endeavor to minister to all ages, all groups, all classes, and all interests within the congregation — without fear or favor.

3. The Pastor shall assume office after his/her name shall have been presented to the entire church by the Pulpit Committee (composed of the staff-Parish Relations Committee, plus three members elected by the church) for a vote. Upon a favorable vote (at least 75 percent), a call shall be extended and the agreements suggested in this instrument shall be made, along with any others which may be necessary.

4. The Pastor shall have the authority to develop comprehensive programs covering all aspects of the church's life. This shall be done within the existing framework of church organization, in cooperation with the duly chosen leaders of the congregation.

5. The Pastor shall maintain an advisory relationship with all groups, boards and committees within the church. He/she shall assist in enlisting, training, and motivating workers, advising on the choice of curriculum materials, providing for meaningful worship experiences, and nurturing spiritual growth.

III. Staff Relationships

1. The Pastor, as chief executive of the church, will counsel together with other members of the church staff during regular staff meetings, held at the discretion of the Pastor.

2. The Pastor will, as much as possible, have regular, announced office hours so that the congregation and its leaders may contact him/her.

3. Associate ministers, secretaries, and other staff (current, or as added) shall work under the direction of and be responsible to the Pastor. Staff additions shall be made by the church upon recommendation by the Pastor and the Church Council.

4. The Pastor is recognized as captain of the team. Loyalty on the part of all staff members is expected. This is not intended, however, to minimize the ministry that the Associate(s) has (have) with the congregation.

5. Should the Pastor resign, it is assumed that other staff members will remain until a new Pastor is secured. Then decisions can be made as to the status of the Staff in consultation with the new Pastor and the Church Council.

IV. Relationships To The Church At Large

1. Loyalty to the historic convictions of the Church of God is expected. The Pastor is expected to be in good standing and full fellowship with the General Assembly of the Church of God, meeting annually at Anderson, Indiana.

2. The Pastor will at all times cooperate actively in promoting the local, area, state, and national work of the Church of God.

3. The Pastor is expected to attend Anderson camp meeting, state camp meeting, Central States Assembly, and other camps, conferences, and conventions as can reasonably be worked into the schedule. He/she shall be permitted two Sundays or three weeks each year to lead revivals, conferences, workshops, and such like.

4. As a professional person, it is important that the Pastor also be a growing person. Therefore, a book allowance from the church will encourage wide reading. A convention allowance will permit attendance at seminars and conferences. Seminary and university courses that would contribute to professional skills and continuing education will be supported.

V. Employment Terms And Agreements

1. The regularly called Pastor shall serve this congregation indefinitely, based on the wishes of the people. Every third year his/her name shall appear on a ballot for an expression from the church. Should the pastor or the congregation desire to take an expression of confidence, or to terminate the relationship, they shall follow the method outlined in the regular church By-laws.

2. The Pastor shall be granted a two-week's vacation at the end of the first and second years of pastoral ministry. With three to seven years of service, he/she shall have three weeks of vacation annually. After seven years of service, the Pastor shall have one month of vacation annually.

3. The church should expect the Pastor to be away from his/her duties for approximately eight weeks (including Sundays) each year for vacations, meetings, conferences and such, with full pay.

4. After seven years of full-time service, the Pastor shall become eligible for a sabbatical leave (at least ten weeks) and a sabbatical every five years thereafter.

5. The Church will support the Pastor in the following amounts which are subject to annual review:

Base Salary	_________________________
Housing Allowance	_________________________
Home Equity Fund	_________________________
Auto Allowance	_________________________
Pension Plan	_________________________
Social Security	_________________________
Life & Health Insurance	_________________________
Convention Allowance	_________________________
Book Allowance	_________________________
Sabbatical Expense Fund	_________________________

6. The Pastor will be expected to take off one full day each week.

7. Adequate office space, equipment, supplies, and secretarial support, will be furnished by the church.

8. A copy of the "Church Manual" will be given to the Pastor. He/she will be expected, as much as possible, to abide by it and to lead the church in its implementation.

9. Should difficulties arise, the Church Council will be available to help work out solutions.

Prepared by: Dwight L. Grubbs, in 1966, at
Anderson School of Theology

Appendix L

Brain Hemisphere Research

We have long known that the human brain contains several sections each with a specialized function, but each vitally related, and working as a whole. More recently, we've discovered how the left and right hemispheres function in personality.

For instance, the left brain is related to critical thinking, logic, sequence, planning, facts and so forth. The right brain is related to creativity, intuition, emotions, imagination and so forth. They are connected and work in harmony. But most persons have one or the other side developed more fully, or experience greater comfort functioning in one or the other hemisphere. This helps to account for the many differences in human perceiving, thinking, acting, and relating.

We know that our educational system is largely left-brain dominated, especially at the graduate level. Right-brain people often feel out of place in schools, and are considered poor ''scholars.'' We also know that about 75 percent of the population tend to be right-brained. So, what is needed? Understanding and appreciation of differences in others. Ministers need to know which their preference is. They need to learn how to relate to other persons effectively, whatever their brain orientation is, allowing them to function in their own unique way.

What does all this have to do with spiritual development? It helps when leaders understand that persons who function more from the left brain tend to be intellectual and volitional, and faith is seen as belief and commitment. Emphasis is upon right thinking and behavior. This person is usually informed and rational, but may appear to be detached (cool) and controlling.

On the other hand, the right-brain person tends to be emotional and intuitive, and faith is seen as trust and discovery. Emphasis is upon right feeling and belonging. This person is usually sensitive and affiliative but may appear to be vacillating and easily offended.

For further reading:

Ashbrook, James B.
    1988 *The Brain and Belief*. Wyndham Hall Press.
Blakeslee, Thomas L.
    1981 *Right-Brain, Left-Brain*. Doubleday Co.
Wink, Walter
    1980 *Transforming Bible Study*. Abingdon. See especially Chapter 8, "Engaging the Other Side of the Brain."
Zdenek, Marilee
    1983 *The Right-Brain Experience: An Intimate Program to Free the Power of Your Imagination*. McGraw-Hill.

Appendix M
Time And Ministry

Since busy pastors generally need help with time management, the following suggestions are provided. The Time Study for Pastors could be used individually, with a group of pastors, or in a local congregation. It is designed to help identify congregational and ministerial expectations.

The "Seventeen Block Plan" suggests ways a pastor's work week may be designed. This plan might be shared with congregational leaders to help them understand what a pastor does with available time.

The following books are recommended for your reading:

Engstrom, Ted W. and R. Alec MacKenzie
1967 *Managing Your Time: Practical Guidelines on the Effective Use of Time.* Zondervan.

Leas, Speed B.
1978 *Time Management: A Working Guide for Church Leaders.* Abingdon.

Mackenzie, R. Alec
1972 *The Time Trap.* AMACOM.

McCabe, Joseph E.
1973 *How to Find Time for Better Preaching and Better Pastoring.* Westminster Press. This book contains some excellent suggestions for saving time in preparing to preach. McCabe describes how to use exchange sermons, repeat sermons, borrowed sermons, modified sermons, and lay sermons, in order to gain an "extra month" of time each year. Very practical!

A Time Study For Pastors

The following list may be used to help determine how time

is being used, how it might be better used, or how much total time is needed to accomplish specific objectives.

Divide the committee or congregation into six groups in order to discuss the specific tasks in their category. Provide each group with one category *only*. Ask them to assign an allotment of time (in hours) that a minister would need in order to do an adequate job in each task, and then a total for their category. Make it realistic, by "averaging out" the work of a typical week. What kind of work-week did the congregation suggest? How realistic is it? Note that Section VI probably ought not be considered part of the pastor's work-week.

I. Preacher — Teacher
1. Sermon preparation   ________
2. Teaching preparation   ________
3. Planning and developing a preaching schedule   ________
4. General Reading   ________
5. Other   ________

                  Total ______

II. Pastoral Care (Ministry With Persons)
1. Calling on the sick (homes, hospitals)   ________
2. Calling on prospective members   ________
3. Counseling (office)   ________
4. Notes, cards, telephoning   ________
5. Home visitation (encouragement, fellowship, etc.)   ________
6. Other   ________

                  Total ______

III. Priestly Functions
1. Planning Worship Services   ________
2. Attendance at Services   ________
3. Weddings and Funerals (including preparation for and follow-up)   ________
4. Other   ________

                  Total ______

IV. Administration
1. Church meetings (board and committees) ______
2. Executive communication (letters, visits, telephone calls, etc.) ______
3. Planning, organizing, promoting ______
4. Newsletter, correspondence ______
5. Reports, preparation for meetings, etc. ______
6. Other ______

Total ______

V. Community Leader
1. Local meetings, speaking engagements, etc. ______
2. Civic organizations and projects ______
3. Ministerial Association ______
4. Other ______

Total ______

VI. Personal And Professional
1. Continuing education (reading, study, writing) ______
2. Professional meetings (local, state, and national) ______
3. Out of town speaking engagements ______
4. Recreation/Exercise ______
5. Personal devotions and enrichment ______
6. Other ______

Total ______

Grand Total ______

(Note: I used this instrument twice while I was a pastor. In each case the Sunday evening congregation reported a work week well in excess of 100 hours would be needed in order to do an adequate job. Obviously, we had something to talk about!)

Hours	Mon.	Tues.	Wed.	Thurs.	Fri.	Sat.
8-12 noon	#1	#4	#7	#9	#12	#15
1-5 p.m.	#2	#5	#8	#10	#13	#16
6-9 p.m.	#3	#6		#11	#14	#17

"The 17-Block Plan"

Suggestion: Use a schedule like this to plan your week as a Pastor. Make the plan idealistic, in that it reflects your priorities and hopes. Wednesday night and Sunday blocks are not included on the assumption that these are "church hours." Indicate *which* blocks will be used for *what purpose*, and fill in the blanks accordingly.

__________ Personal reading and spiritual development
__________ Sermon/teaching preparation
__________ Worship planning
__________ Pastoral care, visitation, etc.
__________ Pastoral administration
__________ Community activities
__________ State/national church activities
__________ Family and free time

__________ _____________________
__________ _____________________
__________ _____________________

17 Blocks (Total)

Weekly Schedule

Time	Mon.	Tues.	Wed.	Thurs.	Fri.	Sat.
8:00						
9:00						
10:00						
11:00						
Noon						
1:00						
2:00						
3:00						
4:00						
5:00						
6:00						
7:00						
8:00						

A Guide To Devotional Bible Study

In order to grow spiritually, seekers need to move beyond *informational* Bible study to *transformational* Bible study. Robert Mulholland, in *Shaped by the Word*, provides clear distinctions and appeals to us to do both.

Informational reading seeks to discover facts and concepts. It objectifies Scripture and tends to be analytical and intellectual in its approach. This approach is more likely to use deductive methods. Formational reading seeks to be more devotional and personal. It deals with mystery and Divine address. It asks the "so what" questions: What, then, may we expect of God? What does God expect of us? This approach is more likely to use inductive methods.

For help in pursuing a devotional approach to Scripture, one might consider:

Arnold, Jeffrey
  1993 *Discovering the Bible for Yourself.* InterVarsity.
Bruggemann, Walter
  1982 *Praying the Psalms.* St. Mary's Press.
Buechner, Frederick
  1977 *Telling the Truth: The Gospel as Tragedy, Comedy and Fairy Tale.* Harper & Row.
Gallagher, Maureen, et al.
  1983 *Praying With Scripture.* Paulist Press.
Jensen, Irving L.
  1963 *Independent Bible Study.* Moody Press.
Leigh, Ronald W.
  1982 *Direct Bible Discovery.* Broadman Press.
Mulholland, M. Robert
  1985 *Shaped by the Word: The Power of Scripture in Spiritual Formation.* Upper Room.
Vos, Howard
  1980 *Effective Bible Study.* Zondervan.
Wink, Walter
  1980 *Transforming Bible Study.* Abingdon.

Appendix O

Sabbatical

This Appendix provides a brief introduction to the idea of sabbatical leaves for pastors. Suggestions for further reading are listed below.

Definition

The word "sabbatical," from sabbath, literally means "seventh," and is related to the Old Testament notion of Sabbath Day (for rest and worship) and Sabbatical Year (for renewal of the cultivated fields). It has come to mean, for many professionals, a leave of absence for purposes of renewal, learning, and growth.

Ideally, the sabbatical leave will provide the time and an environment conducive to reflection, repositioning of perspective, restoration and renewal of inner strengths, along with intellectual and spiritual stimulation.

Possibilities

Sabbaticals work out best when the persons involved design them to meet specific needs. Typically, they occur at seven-year intervals, and last for about six months. However, the variations are unlimited. Some congregations offer sabbaticals after five years of service, perhaps lasting three or four months.

With the current popularity of Doctor of Ministry programs for pastors, many congregations have provided opportunities for further study by permitting sabbatical leaves for doctoral studies. Such a leave may occur during a summer or fall, or, perhaps, both. This would permit an on-campus study experience.

Generally sabbatical leaves are not automatic (every seven years, for example) nor are they necessarily rewards for past service. Rather, they may be considered as investments in a pastor's present and future intellectual, physical, emotional, and spiritual health. Ordinarily, full salary and benefits will be kept in force, except that adjustments may be made if the sabbatical experience provides other significant income for the pastor.

Possible forms that a sabbatical may take, include:

1. Serving in another culture as an interim missionary, teacher, or pastor.

2. Working with disadvantaged persons in a social service agency, community center, or counseling center.

3. Attending seminars, workshops, conferences and such like for personal and professional enrichment.

4. Engaging in a period of intensive study-reflection-prayer at a seminary, house of prayer, or retreat center.

5. Pursuing a major research-writing project related to ministry and church life.

6. Participating in an extensive travel-study experience.

Recommendations

Pastoral ministry calls for total commitment and constant involvement. It is nearly impossible to get away from ministry. So, it is difficult for most pastors to find ways, and schedule the time for relaxation and renewal. But it is not impossible to arrange!

So, pastor, why not ask for what you need? Lay-person, why not suggest it to your pastor? What about next summer? Pastors may find it advantageous to call in an area executive, or visiting evangelist, or seminary professor to help "sell" the congregation on the idea. Without a doubt there are persons available (retired pastors, ministerial students, lay ministers, and so on) who can serve while the pastor is away for a few weeks.

Such a leave will benefit the pastor and the congregation. It might help to prevent burnout, and it might help to avoid the necessity of a pastoral change.

For Further Reading

Bullock, A. Richard
    1987 *Sabbatical Planning.* Alban Institute.
Doohan, Leonard
    1990 *Leisure: A Spiritual Need.* Ave Maria Press.
Edwards, Tilden
    1982 *Sabbath Time.* Seabury Press.
Pohl, David C.
    1978 "Ministerial Sabbaticals," *The Christian Ministry.* (Vol. IX, No. 1) p. 8-10.
Swears, Thomas R.
    1991 *The Approaching Sabbath: Spiritual Disciplines for Pastors.* Abingdon Press.

Selected Bibliography

I. History And Theology Of Spirituality

Alexander, Donald L.
  1988 *Christian Spirituality: Five Views Of Sanctification*, InterVarsity Press.
Bloesch, Donald
  1968 *The Crisis Of Piety: Essays Toward A Theology Of The Christian Life*. Eerdmans.
  1980 *The Struggle Of Prayer*. Harper and Row.
Bosch, David J.
  1979 *A Spirituality Of The Road*. Herald Press.
Bouyer, Louis, et al.
  1963 *A History Of Christian Spirituality*, Vol. I. Seabury Press.
  1968 *A History Of Christian Spirituality*, Vol. II. Seabury Press.
  1969 *A History Of Christian Spirituality*, Vol. III. Seabury Press.
Buttrick, George A.
  1942 *Prayer*. Abingdon Press.
Cox, Michael
  1985 *Handbook Of Christian Spirituality*. Harper and Row.
Edwards, Denis
  1983 *Human Experience Of God*. Paulist Press.
Gannon, Thomas M.
  1984 *The Desert And The City: An Interpretation Of The History Of Christian Spirituality*. Loyola University Press.
Groff, John W.
  1979 *The Mystic Journey*. Forward Movement Publications.
Hall, Thor
  1969 *A Theology Of Christian Devotion*. The Upper Room.
Harkness, Georgia
  1973 *Mysticism: Its Meaning And Message*. Abingdon.
Haughton, Rosemary
  1972 *The Theology Of Experience*. Newman Press.
Holmes, Urban T.
  1980 *A History Of Christian Spirituality*. Seabury Press.
Johnson, Ben C.
  1987 *To Will God's Will*. Westminster.
Johnston, William
  1978 *The Inner Eye Of Love*. Collins.
Jones, Kenneth E.
  1985 *Commitment To Holiness*. Warner Press.
Kelsey, Morton
  1972 *Encounter With God*. Bethany Fellowship.

Kinghorn, Kenneth C.
  1975 *Fresh Wind Of The Spirit*. Abingdon Press.
Leech, Kenneth
  1985 *Experiencing God: Theology As Spirituality*. Harper and Row.
Louth, Andrew
  1978 *Theology And Spirituality*. Fairacres Publication #55.
Lovelace, Richard F.
  1979 *Dynamics Of Spiritual Life: An Evangelical Theology Of Renewal*. InterVarsity Press.
Lundin, Roger and Mark Noll (eds.)
  1987 *Voices From The Heart: Four Centuries Of American Piety*. Eerdmans.
Maas, Robin and Gabriel O'Donnell
  1990 *Spiritual Traditions For The Contemporary Church*. Abingdon.
Mc Neill, J. T.
  1952 *A History Of The Cure Of Souls*. SCM Press.
Newbigin, Leslie
  1977 *The Good Shepherd*. Eerdmans.
Pannenberg, Wolfhart
  1983 *Christian Spirituality*. Westminster
Rack, Henry D.
  1969 *20th Century Spirituality*. Epworth Press.
Rahner, Karl
  1984 *The Practice Of Faith: A Handbook Of Contemporary Spirituality*. Crossroads.
Richards, Lawrence O.
  1987 *A Practical Theology Of Spirituality*. Zondervan.
Schaeffer, Francis A.
  1971 *True Spirituality*. Tyndale House.
Senn, Frank
  1986 *Protestant Spiritual Traditions*. Paulist Press.
Sterner, Eugene
  1981 *God's Caring People*. Warner Press.
Toon, Peter
  1987 *From Mind To Heart*. Baker.
Trueblood, Elton
  1936 *The Essence Of Spiritual Religion*. Harper and Brothers.
  1969 *A Place to Stand*. Harper.
Underhill, Evelyn
  1955 *Mysticism*. Meridian.
  1963 *Concerning The Inner Life And The House Of The Soul*. Methuen.
  1976 *The Essentials Of Mysticism And Other Essays*. AMS Press.
  1976 *The Spiritual Life*. Harper and Row.

Wakefield, Gordon J. (ed.)
  1983 *The Westminster Dictionary Of Christian Spirituality*. Westminster Press.
Walker, Scott
  1986 *Where The Rivers Flow: Exploring The Sources Of Faith Development*. Word.
Wood, Richard
  1980 *Understanding Mysticism*. Image/Doubleday.
Yungblut, John R.
  1979 *Discovering God Within*. Westminster Press.
Zdenek, Marilee
  1983 *The Right-Brain Experience: An Intimate Program To Free The Power of Your Imagination*. McGraw-Hill.

II. The Practice Of Spirituality

Bacovcin, Helen (tr.)
  1978 *The Way Of A Pilgrim*. Image Books.
Barry, William J. and William J. Connolly
  1982 *The Practice Of Spiritual Direction*. Seabury Press.
Bloom, Anthony
  n.d. *Beginning To Pray*.
Bonhoeffer, Dietrich
  1954 *Life Together*. Harper and Row.
Brueggemann, Walter
  1982 *Praying The Psalms*. St. Mary's Press.
Clemmons, William P.
  1987 *Discovering The Depths*. Broadman.
Cousins, Norman
  1979 *Anatomy Of An Illness*. Bantam Books.
  1983 *The Healing Heart*. Avon Books.
Culligan, Kevin G.
  1983 *Spiritual Direction: Contemporary Readings*. Living Flame Press.
Dibbert, Michael T. and Frank B. Wickern
  1985 *Growth Groups*. Zondervan.
Dodd, Robert V.
  1985 *Praying The Name Of Jesus*. The Upper Room.
Doohan, Leonard
  1990 *Leisure: A Spiritual Need*. Ave Maria Press.
Dunnam, Maxie
  1974 *The Workbook Of Living Prayer*. The Upper Room.
  1979 *The Workbook Of Intercessory Prayer*. The Upper Room.
  1982 *Alive In Christ: The Dynamic Process Of Spiritual Formation*. Abingdon.
  1984 *The Workbook On Spiritual Disciplines*. The Upper Room.
Dyckman, Katherine, and Patrick Carroll
  1981 *Inviting The Mystic, Supporting The Prophet: An Introduction To Spiritual Direction*. Paulist Press.

Edwards, Tilden
  1977 *Living Simply Through The Day*. Paulist Press.
  1980 *Spiritual Friend: Reclaiming The Gift Of Spiritual Direction*. Paulist Press.
Foster, Richard J.
  1978 *Celebration Of Discipline*. Harper and Row.
  1981 *Freedom Of Simplicity*. Harper and Row.
Gallagher, Maureen, et. al.
  1983 *Praying With Scripture*. Paulist Press.
Gatta, Julia
  1986 *Three Spiritual Directors For Our Time*. Crowley.
Green, Thomas H.
  1984 *Weeds Among The Wheat: Discernment, Where Prayer And Action Meet*. Ave Maria Press.
Harper, Steve
  1983 *Devotional Life In The Wesleyan Tradition*. The Upper Room.
Hart, Thomas N.
  1980 *The Art Of Christian Listening*. Paulist Press.
Hinson, E. Glenn
  1968 *Seekers After A Mature Faith*. Word.
  1974 *A Serious Call To A Contemplative Life Style*. Westminster Press.
Jones, Alan
  1982 *Exploring Spiritual Direction: An Essay On Christian Friendship*. Seabury Press.
Keen, Sam and James Fowler
  1978 *Life Maps: Conversations On The Journey Of Faith*. Word.
Keirsey, David and Marilyn Bates
  1984 *Please Understand Me: An Essay On Temperament Styles*. Prometheus Nemesis Books.
Kelsey, Morton
  1976 *The Other Side Of Silence: A Guide to Christian Meditation*. Paulist Press.
  1983 *Companions On The Inner Way*. Crossroads.
Klug, Ronald
  1982 *How To Keep A Spiritual Journal*. Thomas Nelson Publishers.
Larson, Bruce
  1971 *No Longer Strangers*. Word.
Leech, Kenneth
  1971 *Soul Friend*. Harper and Row.
  1986 *Spirituality And Pastoral Care*. Sheldon Press.
Massey, James E.
  1985 *Spiritual Disciplines*. Francis Asbury Press.
May, Gerald
  1982 *Care Of Mind, Care Of Spirit: Psychiatric Dimensions Of Spiritual Direction*. Harper and Row.

Merton, Thomas
    1948 *Seeds Of Contemplation*. Dell Books.
    1960 *Spiritual Direction And Meditation*. The Liturgical Press.
    1961 *New Seeds Of Contemplation*. New Directions.
    1972 *Seeds Of Contemplation*. Dell Books.
Michael, Chester P. and Marie C. Norrisey
    1984 *Prayer And Temperament*. The Open Door.
Miller, William A.
    1981 *Make Friends With Your Shadow: How To Accept And Use Positively The Negative Side Of Your Personality*. Augsburg.
Mulholland, Robert
    1985 *Shaped By The Word: The Power Of Scripture In Spiritual Formation*. The Upper Room.
Murray, Andrew
    1984 *The Inner Life*. Whitaker House.
Muto, Susan
    1977 *The Journey Homeward*. Dimension.
Myers, Isabel
    1982 *Gifts Differing*. Consulting Psychologists Press.
Nemeck, Francis and Marie Coombs
    1982 *Contemplation*. Michael Glazier.
Neufelder, Jerome and Mary Coelho
    1982 *Writings In Spiritual Direction*. Seabury Press.
Nouwen, Henri
    1975 *Reaching Out: The Three Movements Of The Spiritual Life*. Doubleday and Company.
    1977 *The Living Reminder*. Copyright 1977 by The Seabury Press. Harper Collins Publishers Inc.
    1980 *The Way Of The Heart: The Desert Fathers And Contemporary Ministry*. Seabury.
    1981 *Making All Things New: An Invitation To The Spiritual Life*. Harper and Row.
Oates, Wayne E.
    1984 *Your Right To Rest*. Westminster.
O'Connor, Elizabeth
    1963 *Call To Commitment*. Harper and Row.
    1968 *Journey Inward, Journey Outward*. Harper and Row.
Paulsell, William
    1976 *Taste And See: A Personal Guide To The Spiritual Life*. The Upper Room.
Peck, Scott
    1978 *The Road Less Traveled: A New Psychology Of Love, Traditional Values, And Spiritual Growth*. Simon and Schuster.

Postema, Don
    1983 *Space For God: The Study And Practice Of Prayer And Spirituality.*
        Board of Publications of the Christian Reformed Church.
Powell, John
    1971 *Why Am I Afraid To Tell You Who I Am?* Argus Communications.
    1974 *The Secret Of Staying In Love.* Argus Communications.
Progoff, Ira
    1975 *At A Journal Workshop.* Dialogue House.
Santa-Maria, Maria L.
    1983 *Growth Through Meditation And Journal Writing: A Jungian Per-
        spective On Christian Spirituality.* Paulist Press.
Seamonds, David A.
    1981 *Healing For Damaged Emotions.* Victor Books.
Seifert, Harvey
    1981 *Explorations In Meditation And Contemplation.* The Upper Room.
Simons, George F.
    1978 *Keeping Your Personal Journal.* Paulist Press.
Smith, Gregory
    1984 *The Fire In Their Eyes: Spiritual Mentors For The Christian Life.*
        Paulist Press.
Steere, Douglas
    1964 *On Beginning From Within.* Harper and Row.
    1982 *Together In Solitude.* Crossroads.
Thornton, Martin
    1984 *Spiritual Direction.* Cowley.
Thurman, Howard
    1963 *Disciplines Of The Spirit.* Harper and Row.
    1974 *The Centering Moment.* Harper and Row.
Vanderwall, Francis W.
    1981 *Spiritual Direction: An Invitation To Abundant Life.* Paulist Press.
Welch, Reuben
    1976 *We Really Do Need Each Other.* Impact Books.
Whiston, Charles F.
    1945 *Instructions In The Life Of Prayer.* Forward Movement Publi-
        cations.
    1972 *Pray: A Study Of Distinctive Christian Praying.* Forward Move-
        ment Publications.
    1985 *Instructions In The Life Of Prayer.* Forward Movement Publi-
        cations.
Wilson, William P.
    1984 *The Grace To Grow: The Power Of Christian Faith In Emotional
        Healing.* Word.

III. Readings In Spirituality
Baille, John
   1955 *A Diary Of Readings.* Scribners.
Benson, Bob and Michael W. Benson
   1985 *Disciplines For The Inner Life.* Word.
Bernanos, Georges
   1954 *The Diary Of A Country Priest.* Doubleday.
Carretto, Carlo
   1972 *Letters From The Desert.* Orbis Books.
Chambers, Oswald
   1935 *My Utmost For His Highest.* Dodd and Mead.
Day, A. E.
   1950 *Discipline And Discovery.* The Upper Room.
Escamilla, Roberto
   1982 *Prisoners Of Hope.* The Upper Room.
Harkness, Georgia
   1945 *Dark Night Of The Soul.* Abingdon.
Job, Rueben and Norman Shawchuck
   1983 *A Guide To Prayer For Ministers And Other Servants.* The Upper
      Room.
Jones, E. Stanley
   1953 *Growing Spiritually.* Abingdon.
   1957 *Christian Maturity.* Abingdon.
Jones, W. Paul
   1981 *The Province Beyond The River.* Paulist.
Keller, Phillip
   1985 *Sea Edge.* Word.
Kelly, Thomas R.
   1941 *A Testament Of Devotion.* Harper and Brothers.
Kepler, Thomas (ed.)
   1977 *The Fellowship Of The Saints: An Anthology Of Christian Devo-
      tional Literature.* Baker Books.
Killinger, John
   1981 *Christ In The Seasons Of Ministry.* Word.
Lawrence, Brother
   1953 *The Practice Of The Presence Of God.* Revell.
Merton, Thomas
   1956 *Thoughts In Solitude.* Farrar, Straus, and Giroux.
Miller, Keith
   1970 *Habitation Of Dragons.* Word.
Murray, Andrew
   1953 *With Christ In The School Of Prayer.* Revell.
Muto, Susan
   n.d. *A Practical Guide To Spiritual Reading.* Dimension Books.

Nouwen, Henri
    1981 *The Genesee Diary: Report From A Trappist Monastery.* Doubleday.
Oldham, Dale
    1970 *Living Close To God.* Warner Press.
Payne, Richard J. (ed.)
    1978-1985 *The Classics Of Western Spirituality.* Paulist Press.
Powell, John
    1974 *He Touched Me.* Argus Communications.
Studdert-Kennedy, G. A.
    1951 *The Best Of Studdert-Kennedy.* Hodder and Stoughton.
Swindoll, Charles R.
    1983 *Growing Strong In The Seasons Of Life.* Multnomah Press.
Thurman, Howard
    1961 *The Inward Journey.* Friends United Press.
van Kaam, Adrian
    1974 *Spirituality And The Gentle Life.* Dimension Books.
Wangerin, Walter
    1984 *Ragman And Other Cries Of Faith.* Harper and Row.
Wesley, John
    1957 *Devotions And Prayers Of John Wesley.* Baker.
    1968 *A Plain Account Of Christian Perfection.* Beacon Hill Press.

IV. Spirituality And Ministry

Cavanagh, Michael E.
    1986 *The Effective Minister: Psychological And Social Considerations.* Harper and Row.
Cox, Robert G.
    1985 *Do You Mean Me, Lord? The Call To Ordained Ministry.* Westminster.
Cully, Iris V.
    1984 *Education For Spiritual Growth.* Harper and Row.
Dale, Robert
    1986 *Pastoral Leadership.* Abingdon.
Demaray, Donald
    1983 *Watch Out For Burnout.* Baker.
Faucett, Robert and Carol Faucett
    1987 *Personality And Spiritual Freedom.* Image Books.
Fenhagen, James
    1978 *More Than Wanderers: Spiritual Disciplines For Christian Ministry.* Seabury Press.
    1981 *Ministry And Solitude.* Seabury Press.
Gunsaulus, Frank W.
    1911 *The Minister And The Spiritual Life.* Fleming H. Revell.

Holmes, Urban T.
  1982 *Spirituality For Ministry*. Harper and Row.
Johnson, Ben C.
  1988 *Pastoral Spirituality*. Westminster Press.
Kemper, Robert G.
  1979 *The New Shape Of Ministry: Taking Accountability Seriously*. Abingdon.
MacDonald, Gordon
  1985 *Ordering Your Private World*. Thomas Nelson.
McBurney, Louis
  1977 *Every Pastor Needs A Pastor*. Word.
Moreman, William
  1984 *Developing Spiritually And Professionally*. Westminster.
Nelson, William R.
  1988 *Ministry Formation For Effective Leadership*. Abingdon.
Neuhaus, Richard J.
  1979 *Freedom For Ministry: A Critical Affirmation Of The Church And Its Mission*. Harper and Row.
Nouwen, Henri
  1971 *Creative Ministry*. Doubleday & Co.
  1972 *The Wounded Healer*. Doubleday & Co.
  1989 *In The Name Of Jesus: Reflections On Christian Leadership*. Crossroads.
Palmer, Parker J.
  1983 *To Know As We Are Known: A Spirituality Of Education*. Copyright 1983 by Parker J. Palmer. Harper and Row.
Paul, Cecil R.
  1981 *Passages Of A Pastor*. Zondervan.
Smith, Fred
  1984 *You And Your Network*. Word.
Swears, Thomas R.
  1991 *The Approaching Sabbath: Spiritual Disciplines For Pastors*. Abingdon Press.
Warlick, Harold C.
  1982 *How To Be A Minister And A Human Being*. Judson Press.

V. Others

Arnold, Jeffrey
  1993 *Discovering The Bible For Yourself*. InterVarsity.
Barlow, Brian C.
  1983 "Theology And Ministry In The Thought Of Henri J. M. Nouwen: A Review And Analysis Of His Writings," (Unpublished Master's Thesis, Anderson School Of Theology).
Braga, James
  1981 *How To Prepare Bible Messages*. Multnomah Press.

Cook, Jerry
    1979 *Love, Acceptance And Forgiveness.* Regal Books.
Engston, Ted W.
    1989 *The Fine Art Of Mentoring.* Woglemuth and Hyatt.
Johnson, Susanne
    1989 *Christian Spiritual Formation In The Church And Classroom.*
        Abingdon.
Jones, Alan
    1980 "Spirituality and Theology," *Review For Religious,* Vol. 39.
Kinlaw, Dennis F.
    1985 *Preaching In The Spirit.* Zondervan.
Koller, Charles W.
    1962 *Expository Preaching Without Notes.* Baker.
Oden, Thomas C.
    1983 *Pastoral Theology: Essentials Of Ministry.* Harper and Row.
Oswald, Roy M.
    1991 *Clergy Self-Care: Finding A Balance For Effective Ministry.* Alban Institute.
Petersen, Herbert and Fern
    1978 *Equality Marriage.* Revell.
Traina, Robert A.
    1952 *Methodical Bible Study.* Asbury Theological Seminary.
Wink, Walter
    1980 *Transforming Bible Study.* Abingdon.
Wuellner, Flora S.
    1991 *Prayer, Stress And Our Inner Wounds.* Upper Room.
    1992 *Heart Of Healing, Heart Of Light.* Upper Room.